FIELD GUIDE TO HAPPINESS

Field Guide to Happiness

The Go-To Guide to Create Happiness and Live A Magical Life

ERIN CHAVEZ

Cover Design by: Ellie Chavez

Windy Day Publishing

First Printing, 2022

Print ISBN: 979-8-9861635-0-5
Ebook ISBN: 979-8-9861635-1-2

Library of Congress Control Number: 2022911610

Windy Day Publishing

Medical Disclaimer
I am not a doctor. Therefore, this book is for informational purposes only and should not be taken as medical advice.

Legal Disclaimer
I am not a lawyer. This book is for informational purposes only and should not be taken as legal advice.

Financial Disclaimer
I am not a financial consultant. This book is for informational purposes only and should not be considered financial advice.

Dedication

Dedicated to every woman who is ready to strip off the labels life has given us, bare her unique self to the mirror, and live her life for only her. For when one of us lives in such a way, we hold the hands of those that come after us, and not only will our personal lives flower, but the entire world will be enchanted with a floral aroma.

"I am woman phenomenally.
Phenomenal woman, that's me."
~ Maya Angelou

Contents

Copyright   iv

Dedication   v

Introduction   1

Bonuses   4

How To Use This Book   7

SECTION 1 - GET HAPPY!

Daily Intentions   14

January   16

February   18

March   20

April   22

May   24

June   26

July   28

August   30

September   32

October   34

November   36

December   38

Magic Recipes   41

Dear Future Me   42

See Ya, Sucker   43

Sticky Sweet   44

Oh, Yes, Please!   46

Plant a Wish   47

Bad Neighbor   48

Charge it Up!   49

The Money Tree   50

Bag O' Confidence!   51

Happy Salts   52

Ommmm   53

Vibin'   54

Full 'Steem' Ahead   55

Root Chakra Balancer   56

Sacral Chakra Balancer   58

Solar Plexus Chakra Balancer   60

Heart Chakra Balancer   62

Throat Chakra Balancer   64

Third Eye Chakra Balancer   66

Crown Chakra Balancer   68

Happiness Boosters! 72

Popular Boosters 74

Do for Others 91

Self Love Boosters 98

SECTION 2 — CONVEY YOUR DESIRES

Visualizations 113

Finding Happiness Visualization 114

Money Flows to Me Visualization 118

Free to be Me Visualization 122

Living Peace & Joy Visualization 126

Life's Balance Visualization 130

My Highest & Best Potential for Fulfillment Visualization 134

The Confidence Critter Visualization 138

Have Fun! Visualization 141

Today I Am Mindful Visualization 144

Give Love. Receive Love. Visualization 148

I Am Health Visualization 152

Affirmations 157

List of Affirmations 158

SECTION 3 - GO-TO PRACTICES

Ho'oponopono 170

Brain Dump Pages 174

Journaling 178

Journaling Prompts   180

Future Journaling   186

Future Journaling Prompts   188

Visualization   195

Visualization Menu   199

Planning   203

Planning Example   204

Feel Your Way   208

Self Expression   212

Gratitude   216

SECTION 4 - REFERENCE

Emotions Chart   225

Energy and Vibration   229

Music and Energy   231

Universal Laws   236

Chakras   241

Chakra Check-In   243

Root Chakra   244

Sacral Chakra   246

Solar Plexus Chakra   248

Heart Chakra   250

Throat Chakra   252

Third Eye Chakra   254

Crown Chakra   256

Divination   260

In Conclusion   265
Recommended Reading   267

Introduction

Imagine yourself sitting around a small, enclosed fire on a tall deck close enough to the ocean, and you can hear the waves lapping down below. You are surrounded by your most loved people, good music, and you are all laughing and immersed in conversation while drinking your favorite drinks and eating your favorite foods.

Then one of your friends holds up their glass for a toast. They all toast you and your generosity for funding this entire getaway. Cheers to you abound as the flickering light from the fire dances across everyone's faces. Finally, one of your friends' faces takes on a serious look, and they say to you, "Please tell us how you did it, how you turned your life around SO much. We all want in on your secret."

You look at them with only love in your eyes and say, "I decided to be happy, and I did it."

**

Could it be that simple? Just by *deciding* to be happy, will you live a wondrous life? By *deciding to be happy, you end up with a* life that exceeds anything you currently think is possible?

Yes.

When you make your happiness a priority in your life, you will notice when you are not happy.

1

When you notice you are not happy, you will find something to make you feel better and happier.

The more you do this, the more you keep noticing and reaching for happiness, the happier you will become overall.

Overall, the happier you are, the better and better your life will become.

At that point, a magical force overcomes you. I don't know what it is or what to call it. Some call it God; some call it the Universe, Source, or divine will. Whatever *it* is, will notice that you want to be happy and that you are willing to do whatever you need to do to be happy. This magic will then swoop in and assure that you are happy with every wish you could ever desire or something better.

**

Many people say you should set a goal for something you want.

"I will earn $500,000 this year."

"I will lose 30 pounds in 6 months."

That's unnecessary. There is only one ultimate goal to strive towards — the goal of happiness. When we pursue happiness in every corner of our lives, we will receive happiness in every corner of our lives. When we receive happiness, we receive anything that could make us happy! From big money to health, the kiss of the morning sun upon your skin, and the smile a puppy brings to your face. Everything.

**

It is my biggest hope that you will carry this book with you at all times. If you need a quick pick-me-up, it will be there for you. If you need an idea to bring you happiness, it will be there for you. If you are simply looking for a reminder to choose happiness, it will be there for you.

**

You don't need this book if you can do a few things. Know what you want. (Complete and utter happiness.) Visualize you being the happiest you can imagine daily. Do things daily that make you happy until you live in a state of almost continual happiness. (Nobody is happy 100% of the time, and that's okay.)

The fact is, though, we have consumed ourselves with things that don't make us happy. Most of all, we've conditioned our minds to preoccupy ourselves from happiness. That is why this book is so vital. It will be your go-to resource to feel better and better until you reach happiness. It is filled with ideas for you to pick from, so you can always do something that feels good to you at the moment you need it most.

Bonuses

Not only do you have this book as a phenomenal resource, but there are additional bonuses for you as well.

You can find those at ErinChavez.com/FGTHBonus.

List of Bonuses:
Finding Happiness Visualization
Money Flows to Me Visualization
Free to be Me Visualization
Living Peace & Joy Visualization
Life's Balance Visualization
My Highest & Best Potential Visualization
The Confidence Critter Visualization
Have Fun Visualization
Today I Am Mindful Visualization
Ancient Solfeggio Scale 396 Hz
Ancient Solfeggio Scale 417 Hz
Ancient Solfeggio Scale 528 Hz
Ancient Solfeggio Scale 639 Hz
Ancient Solfeggio Scale 741 Hz
Ancient Solfeggio Scale 852 Hz
Binaural Beats Delta
Binaural Beats Theta
Binaural Beats Alpha
Binaural Beats Beta

Binaural Beats Gamma
The Emotions Chart PDF in full color
Goal Planning Sheet PDF
Weekly Planner Sheets PDF
Ho'oponopono Print-offs PDF
Visualization Menu Sample PDF
List of Ways to Feel Good PDF
Pendulum Board PDF
And More

"To begin living like you've never lived before,
begin living like you've never lived before."
~ Mike Dooley

NOTES, THOUGHTS & IDEAS

_____
_____
_____
_____
_____
_____
_____
_____
_____
_____
_____
_____
_____
_____
_____
_____
_____
_____
_____
_____
_____
_____
_____

HAPPINESS FACT
Freedom makes us happier than money!

How To Use This Book

First and foremost, use this book in a way that fits you! If it feels good to you, you're doing it right.

With that being said, there are four main sections to this book and several goodies in each section.

Section One: Get Happy!

If you want to *do* something, section one is for you.

Section Two: Convey Your Desires

If you want to *create* something in your mind, section two is for you.

Section Three: Go-To Practices

If you want something to *incorporate* into your life, or even just your day, that will further you on your path, this section is for you.

Section Four: Reference

If you are looking for *references/general knowledge*, section four is for you.

Make no bones about it, though - this is your book to use how you see fit! So, if you see something that spurs an idea for you - go with the idea! Have fun, enjoy, and allow happiness to flow!

Online

On social media, make sure to tag pictures of you being happy with **#fgthbook**. This way we can all find each other and build our Happiness Family!

NOTES, THOUGHTS & IDEAS

_____
_____
_____
_____
_____
_____
_____
_____
_____
_____
_____
_____
_____
_____
_____
_____
_____
_____
_____
_____
_____

Section 1 - Get Happy!

Are you ready to do things that will make you happy?! You're in the right spot! You may notice items are repeated throughout this Get Happy section. This is intentional! Sometimes the way something is presented can bring on an entirely new perspective, or you may pick them on a day you need to see it. If you keep coming across the same type of message, that is no accident. Look at that and ask why it's important for you to know that information.

Daily Intentions

Hello, day! In this part, there are 365 daily intentions for you to read, remember, and implement throughout the day. You can go day by day or just open it to any day and read whichever one your eyes land on. Some of them are fun, and some may stretch your awareness level, but they all are designed to get you and your thinking on the happy side of things.

Magic Recipes

If you want a simple activity laid out in a fun way, you'll love these Magic Recipes! In addition, these Magic Recipes are great to share with friends so that you can do them together!

Happiness Boosters

Boda-Boom! This is a MEGA list of scientifically & meta-physically proven things that will create more happiness within you! Seriously. Nearly everything ever written about how to be happy is included in the Happiness Boosters. You'll find Popular Boosters, Do for Others Boosters, and Self-Love boosters.

"Let us make our future now,
and let us make our dreams tomorrow's reality.
~ Malala Yousafzai

NOTES, THOUGHTS & IDEAS

_____
_____
_____
_____
_____
_____
_____
_____
_____
_____
_____
_____
_____
_____
_____
_____
_____
_____
_____
_____
_____

HAPPINESS FACT:
More light will make you happier!

Daily Intentions

Hello, day! In this part, there are 365 daily intentions for you to read, remember, and implement throughout the day. You can go day by day or just open it to any day and read whichever one your eyes land on. Some of them are fun, some may make you wonder why you are doing them (there's always a reason), and some may stretch your awareness level, but they are all designed to get you and your thinking on the happy side of things.

NOTES, THOUGHTS & IDEAS

_____
_____
_____
_____
_____
_____
_____
_____
_____
_____
_____
_____
_____
_____
_____
_____
_____
_____
_____
_____
_____
_____
_____

January

1. Today, I smile. I smile a lot!
2. Today, I remember my breath. I focus on my breath to bring me into the present moment.
3. Today, I will take one small step to reach my goal.
4. Today, I live happily because happiness is my purpose.
5. Today, I will make sure to drink plenty of water and ask myself if this is something I can always do.
6. Today, I do something to brighten my day.
7. Today, I embrace whatever happens and live fully.
8. Today, I will do something for somebody else that makes them happy.
9. Today, I notice all the good in my life.
10. Today, I visualize myself being exuberantly happy for 4 minutes.
11. Today, I will write a poem about how great I am.
12. Today, I do something simply because it feels good.
13. Today, I will do something nice for an animal.
14. Today, I will look up the #1 song for the year I was born and dance like crazy!
15. Today, I will keep a list of things I'm grateful for.
16. Today, I look inside myself and notice what I feel.
17. Today, I will be of service to someone.
18. Today, I will learn a new word or phrase and use it as often as possible this year.

19. Today, I give only the good parts of me, knowing that what I give, I get back.
20. Today, I will do something different to my appearance. (Does not need to be permanent!)
21. Today, I allow myself to feel the emotions that are natural for me, and they are all centered around love.
22. Today, I will come up with two beautiful things that will help me take care of myself.
23. Today, I will curate a feel-good playlist and share it with a friend.
24. Today I will give a compliment to somebody!
25. Today, I will decide what I want and develop the steps to make it happen!
26. Today, I will drink a green drink in observance of Green Drink Day!
27. Today, I fiercely love those I love, and I let them know it!
28. Today, I *am* the light and focus on all the possibilities because anything is possible.
29. Today, I will learn something I didn't know about a friend or coworker.
30. Today, I will look up a place I want to go and pick a must-go-to business.
31. Today, I will research something that I've been apprehensive about learning. (Like how to become what you most want to be, how to take your dream vacation, or something similar.)

February

1. Today, I will realize that most thoughts I think are automatic and up for debate.
2. Today, I will write a love letter to myself because I am freaking awesome!
3. Today, I compliment others! The more people I compliment, the better!
4. Today, I will take one small step to reach my goal.
5. Today, I don't hold a grudge because I don't know what others are going through.
6. Today, I will do something a little mischievous that is fun and makes me happy!
7. Today, I allow my spirit to lead the way with peace, love, and happiness.
8. Today, I will do something that scares me a little bit.
9. Today, I ask myself what I could release to simplify my life.
10. Today, I allow my natural state — to be one with everything. Love abounds!
11. Today, I will ask somebody for advice that will help me attain a goal.
12. Today, I will get myself a small treat.
13. Today, I will do my best to boost someone's self-esteem.
14. Today, I focus on love, and love will come to me.
15. Today, I think good thoughts and well wishes about anybody I interact with.

16. Today, I will treat myself to a small indulgence.
17. Today, I will purposefully look at a situation differently than before.
18. Today, I will help promote somebody's small business.
19. Today, I will realize that I create my own reality. What do I want?
20. Today, I will live my life like I am the most confident yet humble person alive!
21. Today, I will show myself self-love - however that looks to me.
22. Today, I will notice my posture. I shake myself loose when I'm tight and allow natural alignment.
23. Today, I will pick one book of mine to give to a friend or co-worker (even the library).
24. Today, I affirm that I can do all things because I am a being of light.
25. Today, I will go out of my way to help somebody else.
26. Today, I will do something nice for my neighbor.
27. Today, I remind myself that miracles are a normal part of everyday life, and I look for them.
28. Today, I dedicate 5 minutes to focusing on my breathing.
29. Today I look for somebody who has a birthday today, and I celebrate them somehow!

March

1. Today, I live simply to experience life from my higher self's perspective.
2. Today, I will take the time to enjoy my food fully.
3. Today, I will take one small step to reach my goal.
4. Today, I will do something different and fun!
5. Today, I see the world how I want to see it, not how everybody else sees it.
6. Today, I will give an anonymous letter to somebody to let them know how great they are.
7. Today, I let go of anything that is not happiness, peace, joy, or love.
8. Today, I will listen when somebody talks to me without coming up with something to say.
9. Today, I use my magic wand to transform everything into goodness! (This is a lot of fun!)
10. Today, I walk in light and notice the light in others.
11. Today, I will get a pen and paper and write a new story for myself. I can be anything I want to be!
12. Today, I will find some way to support a local artist.
13. Today, I will look up how to do (and do) an easy numerology reading for myself.
14. Today, I look for reasons to compliment others, and I tell them the compliment!
15. Today, I will act happy — no matter what!

16. Today, I make sure to listen to music that speaks to my spirit and makes me feel great!
17. Today, I will wear green to celebrate St. Patrick's Day!
18. Today, I will write down five different ways I can approach one problem in my life.
19. Today, I think of ways I can simplify my life.
20. Today, I tell myself what I want and accept nothing less!
21. Today, I celebrate the change of seasons!
22. Today, I decide what I want, let it go, and choose to simply be happy.
23. Today, I will compliment three people, either in person, by mail, or online.
24. Today, I allow myself 5 minutes to gaze out of the window and notice the beauty surrounding me.
25. Today, I give my body some attention in whatever way feels good.
26. Today, I will make up my own holiday, celebrating something good I've done in my life.
27. Today, I realize that I am in charge of my life and future, and I'm excited about the possibility!
28. Today, I will decide to get over something small that I've held onto for too long.
29. Today, I repeat, "I am meant for perfect happiness!"
30. Today, I will deep clean something for 10 minutes.
31. Today, I focus on my breathing. I breathe in through my nose for 5 seconds and out for 10 seconds.

April

1. Today, I will pull a great, fun prank on somebody!
2. Today, I remember a memory that makes me laugh, and I tell at least one person!
3. Today, I remember that my thoughts and beliefs create my life.
4. Today, I live by the knowledge that it is my birthright to be happy!
5. Today, I realize that whatever I perceive to be true is based on my personal beliefs and thoughts.
6. Today, I will take one small step to reach my goal.
7. Today, I honor my day. Good, bad, or so-so, it always has something to teach me.
8. Today, I celebrate the diversity around me by supporting a minority-owned business.
9. Today, I think of one thing to make my home feel more alive!
10. Today, I live in the vibration of love so that new answers will show up for me.
11. Today, I empower a woman with uplifting words of encouragement.
12. Today, I allow bad thoughts and beliefs to disappear and the magic to shine.
13. Today, I will learn an Irish dance to celebrate World Irish Dancing Week.

14. Today, I will draw a bird, a frog, or a tree. Then, doodles all around it, making a fun picture.
15. Today, I will take a moment to notice how it feels when my feet hit the ground while I walk.
16. Today, I will clean out my pantry and get rid of the old food or food I no longer want.
17. Today, I look beyond the material world and wonder what else might be there.
18. Today, I will laugh at the crazy (and it's all crazy)!
19. Today, I will write down everything that stresses me out and safely burn it (or ruin it somehow).
20. Today, I read something that feels good.
21. Today, I ask my angels for help in whatever way feels good to me.
22. Today, I will celebrate Mother Earth in a way that feels good to me.
23. Today, I put my phone down and focus on something else for the rest of the day.
24. Today, I will high-five as many people as I can!
25. Today, I devote myself to happiness and see the love in everything.
26. Today, I offer my unique gifts to somebody.
27. Today, I stare out my window and notice everything going on without making up stories about it.
28. Today, I notice how grateful I am for everything!
29. Today, I will make a wish because it is World Wish Day.
30. Today, I will walk around my home for 5 minutes, grab things I don't want anymore & donate them.

May

1. Today, I celebrate the season of warmth and growth!
2. Today, I take the time to appreciate those I love.
3. Today, I will tell somebody why I love them.
4. Today, I will take 2 minutes to give myself the biggest pep talk EVER in the mirror!
5. Today, I will help an underdog - whether it's a plant, an animal, or a human - I will help.
6. Today, I will take one small step to reach my goal.
7. Today, I will attempt to hold somebody's hand (in a non-weird way!)
8. Today, I will take a purposeful walk, noticing my feet and my breath while walking.
9. Today, I realize I can only live in a state of fear or love. So I will choose the love vibration.
10. Today I will clean a room in my home.
11. Today, I will go to my thoughts and think about all the awesome things I can do on vacation.
12. Today, I will go outside and play! Even if playing looks more like walking, I'll have fun!
13. Today, I will pick a small bouquet of dandelions (or another wildflower) to enjoy inside.
14. Today, I take the time to soak up this life of mine. I will relish in the present!
15. Today, I honor my family in a way that feels good to me.

16. Today, I will stretch my body by starting with my head and stretching all the way to my toes.
17. Today, I count how many beautiful things I see.
18. Today, I will write a list of all the things that make me beautiful, inside and out.
19. Today, I will do something special for myself.
20. Today, I realize that all humans are in this together, and I do what I can to bond us together.
21. Today, I will let my freak flag fly and be the unabashed version of ME!
22. Today, I commit to love.
23. Today, I will do something nice for my neighbor.
24. Today, I use my thoughts to play with what my future will hold!
25. Today, I will tap dance in observance of National Tap Dance Day!
26. Today, I forgive. I forgive others, and I forgive myself. I only love.
27. Today, I eat as many fruits and veggies as possible!
28. Today, I ask my higher self for anything and everything! She will make sure it abounds!
29. Today, I smile! I smile at myself, my pets, and the people I live with, and I smile at strangers!
30. Today, I will create something! Anything — it doesn't matter what it is!
31. Today, I make sure to eat healthy foods for my body, alongside whatever else I might want to eat.

June

1. Today, I will find some way to support somebody in the LGBTQ+ community!
2. Today, I only see my beauty and speak nicely to myself.
3. Today, I write down what I want and put it in an envelope to open in 3 months.
4. Today, I live to radiate my love.
5. Today, I forgive myself for past mistakes, knowing I did the best I could at the time.
6. Today, I intend to see only the beauty that today offers.
7. Today, I will eat at least six servings of produce.
8. Today, I will take one small step to reach my goal.
9. Today, I will see each person as an extension of myself — because they are.
10. Today, I will ask, "what if." What if I actually can do X, Y, or Z?!
11. Today, I realize that my bad thoughts only have power because I allow them to.
12. Today, I am on a quest to get a nice glass of lemonade!
13. Today, I will list things that I feel would make me happy.
14. Today, I will play catch! Even if it's inside, by myself, with a balled-up piece of paper.
15. Today, I look at myself naked and honestly tell myself I am beautiful!
16. Today, I will list five things I like about something or somebody who annoys me.

17. Today, I visualize exactly what I want my life to be. See it as already happening.
18. Today, I will splurge on myself, even if just a little.
19. Today, I give freely that which I desire most!
20. Today, I will be so productive that I will amaze myself!
21. Today, I celebrate the change of seasons!
22. Today, I will create a brand new reality for myself based on my thoughts.
23. Today, I will let go of something that's been bothering me.
24. Today, I ask myself purposeful ways to allow more goodness into my life.
25. Today, I will make something new! Anything from a drawing to a recipe to a friend!
26. Today, I observe the truth about what surrounds me and help where I can.
27. Today, I will celebrate my joy and happiness!
28. Today, I will focus on forgiveness and even try Ho'opono-pono.
29. Today, I will create an elaborate handshake with a friend!
30. Today, I write down who I want to become, and then I start living in ways that will create that new version of me.

July

1. Today, I stay in the present moment while expecting the best.
2. Today, I remind myself that my reality is based on my perception of life.
3. Today, I will take a few minutes to listen to my thoughts. Do I want those thoughts?
4. Today, I'll walk barefoot on the earth to release any negativity I have.
5. Today, I will take one small step to reach my goal.
6. Today, I fling my arms wide open and allow the flow of energy into me!
7. Today, I sit, relax, and feel the breeze and sunshine on my face.
8. Today, I will forgive somebody from my past or present.
9. Today, I will take 5 minutes to clean something really good!
10. Today, I will cheer somebody up who needs it!
11. Today, I see myself as a glowing, glittering person dropping bits of happiness wherever I go.
12. Today, I will figure out how to simplify my life and take the steps needed to implement it.
13. Today, I will write a letter as my future self telling my current day self how great life has become!
14. Today, I will embrace my nudity to celebrate International Nude Day!

15. Today, I will support a small business in whatever way I can.
16. Today, I acknowledge that I can do anything and ask myself where I hold myself back.
17. Today, I will donate something. It doesn't matter what or to whom.
18. Today, I will apologize for something I did that is long overdue.
19. Today, I will say, "I love you" every time I pass a mirror.
20. Tonight, I will look at the moon and marvel in the wonder of all that is.
21. Today, I notice that if my thoughts aren't good, I'm rejecting the love that is me.
22. Today, I will reach out to someone who seems like they need a little something extra.
23. Today, I live beyond my five senses and allow the wonder of what else is before me.
24. Today, I will indulge in self-care in honor of International Self Care Day.
25. Today, I will look in the mirror and compliment myself ... a lot!
26. Today, I will take the time to be by myself, enjoying the solitude.
27. Today, I will make a list of things that I feel would make me happy.
28. Today, I will take the time to enjoy a cool, crisp, refreshing drink thoroughly.
29. Today, I will ask myself who I *really* am — on a deep level — to gain more understanding.
30. Today, I will do everything in my power to allow fun into my life!
31. Today I will dance! I will dance by myself or with somebody else, but I dance as if the music comes from my soul!

August

1. Today, I will find a quick meditation on YouTube and enjoy the break.
2. Today, I acknowledge we are all one — all part of the same light of love.
3. Today, I find the good in each situation.
4. Today, I ask for a sign that I am loved.
5. Today, I proclaim that I am magical, and my thoughts dictate my life!
6. Today, I will take one small step to reach my goal.
7. Today, I will allow happiness to happen all around me!
8. Today, I will answer the question, "To me, happiness is..."
9. Today, I will read a book that I love!
10. Today, I will think about the fact that my soul is residing in this body of mine.
11. Today, I will sit and write for two full pages about whatever comes to mind.
12. Today, I will learn something new.
13. Today, I imagine just how magical I am and have a pep in my step because of that!
14. Today, I will tell my best friend how special they are to me.
15. Today, I talk kindly to myself. All-day!
16. Today, I will sit and observe other people while thinking about what is really important in my life.

17. Today, I will pamper my feet in observance of I Love My Feet Day.
18. Today, I live like I think my higher self wants me to live — not my ego.
19. Today, I will seek to take the perfect picture.
20. Today, I affirm that my idea of a brilliant life is mine for taking.
21. Today, I will take stock of where I am with my health and decide how to feel better.
22. Today, I write a goodbye letter to something I want out of my life.
23. Today, I will relax in a way that is relaxing for me.
24. Today, I will find the strangest music and share it with a friend.
25. Today I will write a letter to an old friend.
26. Today, I allow myself to BE ME!
27. Today, I notice if my ego or the real me is in charge of my thoughts.
28. Today, I repeat: "I AM FREAKING MAGICAL!"
29. Today, I will eat more herbs and less salt to celebrate More Herbs, Less Salt Day.
30. Today, I will acknowledge any grief I'm carrying and repeat the Ho'oponopono prayer.
31. Today, I will do a random act of kindness!

September

1. Today, I will do something that makes me feel alive and wonderful!
2. Today, I will focus on love and happiness. Nothing else matters but love and happiness.
3. Today, I will challenge myself to do something — like doing five squats before using the toilet.
4. Today, I will let go of the reality society has made up, and I will decide my *own* reality!
5. Today, I will make a list of what I want and simple steps to get there!
6. Today, I will take one small step to reach my goal.
7. Today, I will try something different — no matter how big or small.
8. Today, I will visualize myself living the life of my dreams!
9. Today, I purposefully choose love over any negative emotion.
10. Today, I will embrace my weirdness and live it proudly!
11. Today, I will check in with myself and notice how I'm doing.
12. Today, I will encourage somebody.
13. Today, I will write a letter to someone who has died and see if they answer me somehow, someway.
14. Today, I will observe my thoughts and replace negative thoughts with positive thoughts.

15. Today, I will convince myself that what I want is MINE and making its way to me.
16. Today, I will dance like I am the best dancer in the world!
17. Today, I will stay in the present moment as often as possible.
18. Today, I will do something to enhance one of my relationships.
19. Today, I will talk like a pirate! (It's Talk Like A Pirate Day)
20. Today, I will create! I will create anything that feels good to me!
21. Today, I will celebrate the change of seasons!
22. Today, I will do something that I've been putting off.
23. Today, I expect the best.
24. Today, I will learn a simple phrase in sign language.
25. Today, I will notice my personal vibe. Is it what I want it to be?
26. Today, I will write a letter of forgiveness for someone else or myself.
27. Today, I will sit for a moment and find peace within myself.
28. Today, I focus on the good and release any bad.
29. Today, I will have a good cup of coffee to celebrate International Coffee Day.
30. Today, I embrace my weirdness, and I'm empowered by it! I'll show it off for the world to see!

October

1. Today, I catch mean things I say to myself and turn them into something lovely.
2. Today, I will ask for what I want!
3. Today, I take an issue in my life and look at it from a different angle.
4. Today, I pursue happiness down every path.
5. Today, I allow happiness, love, and peace to fill me.
6. Today, I smile and wave at a stranger as if I know them.
7. Today, I will take one small step to reach my goal.
8. Today, I will write down my favorite five things about my partner or future partner.
9. Today, I will be bold, be free, and be me!
10. Today, I realize society does not know the truth. What do I want my truth to be? Anything is possible!
11. Today, I will get funky in whatever way feels good to me!
12. Today, I will allow my thoughts to wander to simply see where they go. If I notice they are going negative, I will steer them toward happiness.
13. Today, I will think about what new habit I want in my life and how to incorporate that habit.
14. Today, I will clean out one drawer and get rid of what I don't need anymore.
15. Today, I will develop a mantra and repeat it throughout the day.
16. Today, I will do something nice for somebody else.

17. Today, I will learn a new word and use it!
18. Today, I focus on what I love — not what I fear.
19. Today, I will take stock of where I am, where I want to be, and take steps to get there.
20. Today, I will write down three things I want others to know about me, and then I will start to show that side of me.
21. Today, I will take a moment to breathe. I allow my exhale to be 2x longer than my inhale.
22. Today, I will do something to make a positive difference in somebody's life.
23. Today, I realize that my health is what I believe it to be.
24. Today, I will take the time to enjoy my food!
25. Today, I will buy a piece of art. (Etsy is a great, inexpensive place to look.)
26. Today, I will take 5 minutes to organize something.
27. Today, I will journal about my strengths and how I can use them in my life.
28. Today, I remember that I have the power to fix anything because I am magical!
29. Today, I will make a checklist of everything I want to get done.
30. Today, I remind myself that I can do anything! I ask for answers and believe in myself.
31. Today, I realize society does not know the truth. What do I want my truth to be? Anything is possible!

November

1. Today, I will catch myself thinking good thoughts.
2. Today, I realize that anything I put after "I AM" is truth to me, and I choose my words wisely.
3. Today, I allow myself to enjoy life thoroughly!
4. Today, I only focus on what I want.
5. Today, I embrace nature! No matter the weather, I enjoy what it has to offer me.
6. Today, I will take one small step to reach my goal.
7. Today, I will go through my home and get rid of things I no longer need.
8. Today, I behave like I already AM the person I want to be.
9. Today, I will get logical and come up with three main things I can do to *be* who I want to be.
10. Today, I will catch myself when I say "should" or "need to," and I will change that statement!
11. Today, I release a belief I no longer want.
12. Today, I will notice everything I am grateful for all day long.
13. Today, I will be kind to others, animals, mother nature, and me to honor World Kindness Day.
14. Today, I focus only on what is good and going right.
15. Today, I notice how the shadows play across the earth.
16. Today, I think about if I were to write a book or start a business, what would it be about?
17. Today, I give love and gratitude to my body!

18. Today, I allow the miracle of love into my life and my body!
19. Today, I will create a challenge for myself.
20. Today, I will do something nice for somebody else.
21. Today, I will write out my ideal week, and I'm not afraid of making it extraordinary!
22. Today, I reevaluate and decide what beliefs I *really* want.
23. Today, I will tell or show somebody my unique talent!
24. Today, I define what my reality is!
25. Today, I take 5 minutes to breathe out all the negativity and breathe in love.
26. Today, I will do a random act of kindness.
27. Today, I write down what I want for my future in the present tense, as if it's already mine.
28. Today, I take the time to visualize that I am pure light, love, and happiness!
29. Today, I write down five obscure things I'm grateful for.
30. Today, I look at recurring issues in my life and see how I could approach them differently.

December

1. Today, I will take 5 minutes to sit outside, without my phone, and simply notice my surroundings.
2. Today, I imagine being bathed in a purple light that is full of love, happiness, and peace.
3. Today, I will take one small step to reach my goal.
4. Today, I claim happiness, fun, joy, and peace and accept nothing less!
5. Today, I allow myself to dazzle, be bold, and be ME!
6. Today, I am on alert to see a bird. I know each bird I see is a confirmation of my innate happiness.
7. Today, I give happiness, love, and peace because the more I give, the more I get!
8. Today, I still myself and ask for the truth of the nature of reality.
9. Today, I will turn off the news and create my own good story.
10. Today, I only pursue happiness.
11. Today, I will gather things at home to donate to a shelter.
12. Today I will call somebody and tell them I am thinking about them.
13. Today, I show up in fullness as my higher self!
14. Today, I will do yoga!
15. Today, I will do something extra nice for myself.
16. Today, I ask for help from the powers that be if I have trouble being happy.

17. Today, I allow myself to visualize things that I can't see with my eyes.
18. Today, I will learn something new.
19. Today, I give love and receive love.
20. Today, I will ask myself, "What if everything turned out just fine"?
21. Today, I relish in the change of the season.
22. Today, I will tidy up my home a little more than usual.
23. Today, I ask my higher self for help, and I stay open to the answers.
24. Today, I will reflect on good memories and share one (or more) with someone.
25. Today, I do one thing — enjoy.
26. Today, I will make a list of new skills I want to learn because they seem enjoyable.
27. Today, I will pick a book to read in January.
28. Today, I release something from my past that no longer serves me.
29. Today, I will make a list of everything I want to accomplish in my life.
30. Today, I will give something my complete focus.
31. Today, I take stock of a year well lived and ask what I want to be different next year.

NOTES, THOUGHTS & IDEAS

_____
_____
_____
_____
_____
_____
_____
_____
_____
_____
_____
_____
_____
_____
_____
_____
_____
_____
_____
_____
_____

Magic Recipes

If you want a simple activity laid out in a fun way, you'll love these Magic Recipes! There *are* a few repetitions between these Magic Recipes and the Happiness Boosters. This is because the way something is presented can bring on an entirely new perspective. These Magic Recipes are great to share with friends so that you can do them together!

Dear Future Me

DEAR FUTURE ME - *To Attain Your Goals*

Ingredients
Pen, Paper, Envelope

Time Involved
15 minutes writing plus 15 minutes planning

Procedure

1. Write a letter to yourself, laying out who you want to become or be one year from now. Write it as if it has already happened, and be grateful to your future self for making it come true!
2. Seal it in an envelope and put the open date on it.
3. Make a plan that you'll do so you will accomplish what is in the letter.
4. Set a reminder so you remember to open in one year from writing.

Notes
You can write several letters to your future self at different yearly intervals - 1 year, two years, five years, ten years, twenty years, etc.!

See Ya, Sucker

SEE YA, SUCKER - *To Let Go of Something*

Ingredients
Pen, paper, black candle, orange or lemon essential oil, or the actual fruit, safe place to burn paper.

Time Involved
20 minutes

Procedure

1. Decide on something you want to let go of in your life.
2. Write that thing on a piece of paper. You can state it generally or write everything you feel.
3. Safely burn it from the flame of a black candle.
4. Either anoint yourself with your essential oil or just your fruit - knowing and feeling you've let it go, and starting fresh.

Notes
You can make this more elaborate by adding daffodils or daisies to display after the burning to signify new beginnings and/or wearing a smoky quartz crystal to neutralize the negative and promote the positive.

Sticky Sweet

STICKY SWEET - *To Improve a Relationship*

Ingredients
Pen, paper, small white candle, glass honey jar

Time Involved
15 minutes plus one week

Procedure

1. Write the name of the person you want the improved relationship with 3x on a piece of paper and write your intention for your relationship.
2. Fold the paper and stick it in the honey while repeating your intention 3x. Make sure your fingers touch the honey when you put the paper in the honey.
3. Lick the honey from your fingers and put the lid on the honey jar.
4. Put the white candle on top of the honey jar, light it and let it burn all the way down.
5. Put the honey jar somewhere hidden for a week.
6. During the week, think pleasant thoughts about the person and repeat your intention.

Notes

Possible Intentions:

I intend to have a joyous relationship with _____.

I intend for the best possible outcome in my relationship with _____.

I intend to have excellent communication with _____.

I intend to feel amazing love toward _____.

Oh, Yes, Please!

OH, YES, PLEASE! - *To Get Something You Want*

Ingredients
A desire, pen, paper, one orgasm (or more!)

Time Involved
10 minutes plus orgasm

Procedure

1. Decide on your desire/intention.
2. Draw a very simple image that depicts your desire.
3. Put the drawing under your pillow.
4. Have an orgasm, and at the peak of your pleasure, imagine in your mind the image you drew.

Notes
It is best to do this *every* time you orgasm until you attain your desire/intention.

Plant a Wish

PLANT A WISH - *To Get Something You Want*

Ingredients
One wish, a pack of flower seeds (or green bean seeds for quickness), a possible pot and soil if it's too cold where you live to plant outside

Time Involved
10 minutes plus however long it takes your seeds to grow

Procedure

1. Decide on a wish for yourself. You might want to write it down so you remember it exactly.
2. Plant your seeds according to package directions.
3. As you're planting, focus on your wish as having come true already.
4. Every day, tell your wish to your seeds.
5. Expect your wish to come true!

Notes
For even more magic, visualize your wish already having come true every day.

Bad Neighbor

BAD NEIGHBOR NO MORE - *To Better a Relationship with Neighbor*

Ingredients
Mirror suitable for the outdoors

Time Involved
2 minutes prep plus 3 minutes a day

Procedure

1. Place the mirror inconspicuously outside, facing your questionable neighbor.
2. For 3 minutes each day, imagine love raining upon your neighbor's house.
3. If you notice negative thoughts about your neighbor, repeat, "We are all one. There is only love."
4. In your mind, shower your neighbor and their home with gold.
5. Continue until your relationship improves with your neighbor.

Notes
If you want to increase the magic, send an anonymous gift to your neighbor and sign the tag, "From Your Caring Neighbor."

Charge it Up!

CHARGE IT UP! *For Health (and a whole lot more)*

Ingredients
Glass of water, intention for health (or any other intention you'd like)

Time Involved
5 minutes

Procedure

1. Fill the glass with water.
2. Hold the glass with both hands, palms on the glass.
3. Say your health intention, knowing you're charging our water with that intention for the present moment and for days to come.
4. Keep your palms on the glass, thinking about and being grateful for your intention and this magic for about 2 minutes while sipping the water until you have finished it all.

Notes
You can use *any* intention. It doesn't need to be health-related!

Repeat this as often as you feel necessary.

The Money Tree

THE MONEY TREE! - *For Money*

Ingredients
A tree you can dig a hole next to, paper, green marker, 8 pennies, an envelope, waxing moon phase.

Time Involved
15 minutes

Procedure

1. Do this outside, under a tree, under a waxing moon phase.
2. Write a believable amount of money you want on the paper with your green marker.
3. Fold your paper 4x and put it in the envelope.
4. Add the 8 pennies to the envelope while saying, "8 pennies for riches to flow, 8 pennies for financial opportunities to grow. So be it."
5. Seal the envelope.
6. Bury the envelope by the tree and thank the tree for growing more money into your life.

Notes
Be on the lookout for financial opportunities!

Bag O' Confidence!

BAG O' CONFIDENCE! - *For Confidence*

Ingredients
Something yellow, rosemary, red jasper, lavender, orange peel, small cloth bag. (Add anything that means confidence to you.)

Time Involved
Varies to find objects plus 5 minutes to put together

Procedure

1. Procure all the items and put in the cloth bag.
2. After all of your items are in the bag, put the bag under your pillow.
3. Each night before going to sleep, imagine you in a power pose - either with your arms behind your head and your feet up on a desk or with your arms raised in victory - pumping them with excitement.
4. Be grateful for your bag of confidence, send it gratitude, and feel it send you back confidence.

Notes
Taking the time to procure the items that go in the bag is part of this magic recipe.

Happy Salts

HAPPY SALTS! - *For Happiness*

Ingredients
1 cup Epsom salt, ½ cup Himalayan pink salt, 20 drops lemon* essential oil, glass jar

Time Involved
5 minutes plus bath

Procedure

1. Put both salts in glass jar and add 20 drops of essential oil.
2. Shake the jar as much as you can.
3. Hold the jar between your palms and imagine the universe beaming happiness through your head, your palms, and into the jar.
4. Take a leisurely bath with as much of your happy salts as you'd like.
5. While bathing, think of all the reasons you have to be grateful and imagine you and your bath water radiating happiness.

Notes
*You can substitute for a non-citrus essential oil if you'd like to be in the sun afterwards (like lavender oil).

Ommmm

OMMMM - *For Inner Peace*

Ingredients

Chamomile, lavender or other herbal tea, Chamomile or lavender candle, timer, journal, and pen

Time Involved

20+ minutes

Procedure

1. Make your tea, and light your candle in a place you won't be disturbed.
2. Set your timer for 10 minutes. Journal about your problems/fears or about how good things are.
3. After timer dings, stop writing and set it for another 10 minutes.
4. Focus on your breath. Breathe in 4 counts. Hold 5 counts. Exhale 8 counts. Do this until your timer dings.
5. Finish your tea and journal if you feel like it.

Notes

This magic recipe is all about feeling peaceful inside. If you have something pressing on your mind, write about it so you can release it! Doing so will allow you to focus on the good.

Vibin'

VIBIN' - *Proof Your Thoughts & Words Matter*

Ingredients
Three identical jars, 3 cups cooked rice, writable tape.

Time Involved
20 minutes prep plus 1 minute every day for ~2 weeks

Procedure

1. Wash and dry all of the jars.
2. Cook the rice.
3. Put equal amounts of rice in each jar and screw on the lids.
4. Write "Love" and "Hate" on the tape and put them each on a jar. Leave one jar blank.
5. Put all three jars where they receive the same amount of sunlight/darkness.
6. Daily, say, "I love you" to the Love jar. Ignore the jar with nothing on it. Say, "I hate you" to the Hate jar.

Notes
If you forget to visit your jars, you can send love to your love jar and send hate to your hate jar. Just imagine you sending the emotion!

Full 'Steem' Ahead

FULL (self-e)STEEM AHEAD - *For Self Esteem*

Ingredients
Sticky notes (or similar), pen or markers, piece of paper

Time Involved
30 minutes

Procedure

1. Fold the paper in half longways. On the left side of the paper, write down all the negative things you say/think about yourself.
2. For each negative thing, write the opposite on the right side of the paper.
3. Tear the sheet in half and throw away the left side.
4. Looking at your positive statements, circle three that you can *really* get behind.
5. Write each one of those three statements on a sticky note and put them up where you'll see them regularly.
6. When you see them, read them & *feel* that they are true!

Notes
Use them as affirmations and repeat these statements to yourself all day.

Root Chakra Balancer

ROOT CHAKRA BALANCER
If You Need to Feel Balanced

Ingredients
Powerful music, Mother Earth, Patchouli, or Cedarwood essential oil

Time Involved
Varies

Procedure

1. Do the root chakra visualization.
2. Put on some powerful, bass-filled music and dance freely! Focus on heavy stomping movements and solid foot movement.
3. If possible, go for a walk barefoot on Mother Earth.
4. Take a shower and give special attention to your feet.
5. Anoint yourself with patchouli or cedarwood oil, knowing those scents will ground you.
6. Do the visualization again.

Notes

Eat red foods like red apples, strawberries, tomatoes, beets, and sweet potatoes (a *root* vegetable).

Good essential oils are cedarwood, patchouli, and sandalwood.

Visualization

Visualize the color red glowing at the base of your spine. See it rotating and growing stronger. Then, see the red light going down through your legs and feet, deep into the earth, grounding you to the center of the earth.

Sacral Chakra Balancer

SACRAL CHAKRA BALANCER
If You Need to Feel Empowered or Creative

Ingredients
Journal, pen, emotion-filled music

Time Involved
Varies

Procedure

1. Do the sacral chakra visualization.
2. Put on some emotion-filled music until you are done journaling.
3. Stretch your hips (the butterfly stretch, for example).
4. Set a timer for 5 minutes, close your eyes, and focus on the flow of your breath.
5. Journal about the following questions:
   ○ What would it/does it look like for me to be empowered by my creativity?
   ○ Am I currently allowing my creativity to flow? How am I allowing that flow, or how do I wish I was allowing the flow?

     ◦ How can I make my sex life better - with a partner
       or by myself?
6. Do the sacral visualization.

Notes
Eat orange foods like oranges, cantaloupe, pumpkin, carrots, and sweet potatoes.

Good essential oils are orange, patchouli and sandalwood.

Visualization
Imagine a glowing orange light glow just below your belly button. Allow the orange glow to rotate and grow bigger while feeling the feelings of generosity, confidence, sexual energy, and creativity. (It's okay if you don't remember them all - just remember what's important to you.) Allow a warm feeling to fill your abdomen.

Solar Plexus Chakra Balancer

SOLAR PLEXUS CHAKRA BALANCER
If You Need Self-Esteem

Ingredients
Warmth/heat, pen, paper

Time Involved
Varies

Procedure

1. Do the solar plexus visualization.
2. When making choices today, make sure they create feelings of personal power for you!
3. Spend time in warm sunlight, a warm bath, or even a heating pad on your abdomen.
4. Do something that creates heat a few inches above your belly button, like crunches, boxing, or cobra pose.
5. Get your pen and paper and create an affirmation* or a mantra that celebrates your personal power!

Notes

Eat yellow foods like bananas, lemons, pineapple, turmeric (creates heat), and ginger (creates heat).

Good essential oils are sandalwood, ylang-ylang, lemongrass, and lavender.

*Examples of affirmations:
I have unlimited power.
I am powerful.
I am love.
I can do anything.

Visualization

Imagine a yellow glow slightly above your belly button. See this yellow glow rotate and feel the warmth it produces. Imagine being playful, reliable, and having a warm, glowing personality. Imagine what it feels like to have good self-esteem. Repeat "I AM WORTHY" until you're ready to end this visualization. Imagine the yellow glow filling your room and your entire life right before you end.

Heart Chakra
Balancer

HEART CHAKRA BALANCER
If You Want More Love in Your Life

Ingredients
Mirror, pen, paper

Time Involved
Varies

Procedure

1. Do the heart chakra visualization.
2. Look into your eyes in a mirror, and say, "I love you." Say it with feeling and repeat it 10-20 times.
3. Write a letter to somebody, forgiving them. You don't need to send it.
4. Make three lists: how you can show more love to yourself, your loved ones, and strangers.
5. Do heart visualization again.
6. Go back to the mirror, look into your eyes, and say, "I love you." Say it with feeling and repeat it 10-20 times.

Notes

Eat green foods like broccoli, Brussel sprouts, celery, green tea, spinach, green apples, and cucumbers.

Good essential oils are rose, jasmine, lavender, sandalwood, and orange.

Visualization

Imagine a green glow in your heart area. Watch as it begins to rotate and glow bigger and bigger. Repeat, "I love myself, I forgive, I love."; and feel the loving vibration of your glowing, rotating green heart chakra. Right before you are ready to end your visualization, imagine the green glow touching those around you and those you love.

Throat Chakra Balancer

THROAT CHAKRA BALANCER
If You Need to Communicate Clearly

Ingredients
Journal, pen, hot herbal tea, timer

Time Involved
Varies

Procedure

1. Do heart chakra visualization.
2. Make some hot tea to pamper your throat chakra.
3. Journal about your needs, desires, and strong opinions.
4. Drop your chin to your chest as far as feels comfortable for as long as you'd like.
5. Drop your left ear to your left shoulder and right ear to your right shoulder for as long as you'd like.
6. Set a timer and do some mindful breathing - even if only for 3 minutes. Simply close your eyes and focus on your breath until your timer goes off.
7. Do heart chakra visualization again.
8. Hum today - a lot!

Notes

Eat blue foods like blueberries and blackberries; and things that will soothe your throat like herbal tea, honey, and bone broth.

Good essential oils are peppermint, eucalyptus, tea tree, and lavender.

Visualization

Imagine a blue glow near your voice box. Watch as it begins to rotate and grow and glow bigger and bigger. Next, begin to move your head and stretch your neck so this glowing, rotating blue color can penetrate every cell in your neck. While stretching, focus on deep inhales and long exhales. Wrap up your visualization by repeating, "I am authentic" until you're ready to end.

Third Eye Chakra Balancer

THIRD EYE CHAKRA BALANCER
If You Want to Improve Your Intuition

Ingredients
White candle, lavender essential oil, timer, notebook, and pen

Time Involved
Varies

Procedure

1. Do third eye chakra visualization.
2. Set a timer for your desired length, light your candle, and simply focus on the flame until your timer goes off.
3. Take a nap! Put your notebook and pen by your nap area. Before you go to sleep, tell yourself you'll remember your dreams/visions. Then, when you wake up, write down what you remember.
4. Take a relaxing bath with lavender essential oil and your white candle. While in the bath, focus on your candle's flame again and do the third eye visualization again.

Notes

Eat purple foods like red onion, red cabbage, blueberries, purple and red grapes, and eggplant.

Good essential oils are lavender and frankincense.

Visualization

Imagine a purple glow between your eyebrows and slightly up from there. Watch as this purple glow grows and rotates. Repeat, "I am imaginative and intuitive. The knowledge of the universe is within me." Imagine your glowing, purple light reaching out as far as you can imagine until you are ready to end your visualization.

Crown Chakra Balancer

CROWN CHAKRA BALANCER
If You Want to Connect with Source

Ingredients
Sage Smudge Stick

Time Involved
Varies

Procedure

1. Do crown chakra visualization.
2. Declutter or clean your home and other spaces. (If you feel overwhelmed by this, just focus on a tiny area.)
3. Sage your home and other spaces.
4. Read a book to further your spiritual journey.
5. Always return to the visualization. Again and again.

Notes
Drink pure water, get fresh air and enjoy the sunlight and moonlight.

Good essential oils are frankincense, rose, and sandalwood.

Visualization

Imagine a violet glow at the top of your head. Watch as the glow grows and begins to rotate. Start to notice your thoughts and then wonder what or who is noticing those thoughts. You might feel a disconnect at that point, and that is perfect. Keep noticing who or what is observing your thoughts. When you're ready to end this visualization, see the purple light envelope your body and say, "I AM LOVE."

NOTES, THOUGHTS & IDEAS

_____
_____
_____
_____
_____
_____
_____
_____
_____
_____
_____
_____
_____
_____
_____
_____
_____
_____
_____
_____
_____
_____
_____

QUOTE
"Happiness isn't what you find at the end of the
road. It's right here, right now."
~ Unknown

NOTES, THOUGHTS & IDEAS

_____
_____
_____
_____
_____
_____
_____
_____
_____
_____
_____
_____
_____
_____
_____
_____
_____
_____
_____
_____
_____
_____
_____

Happiness Boosters!

Boda-Boom! This is a MEGA list of scientifically & meta-physically proven things that will create more happiness within you! Seriously. Nearly everything ever written about how to be happy is included in the Happiness Boosters.

You might notice some boosters are repeated in different ways. This is intentional. Seeing or reading something differently might be all you need for it to touch your heart the way you need it to.

NOTES, THOUGHTS & IDEAS

_____
_____
_____
_____
_____
_____
_____
_____
_____
_____
_____
_____
_____
_____
_____
_____
_____
_____
_____
_____
_____

Popular Boosters

Are you looking for quick and easy recommendations that will bring some happiness and magic into your life? Look no further! These boosters are *all* about you. Some are quick, and others that take more time. It's all about what feels good to you.

Get Some Flowers
The smell of flowers and seeing them will increase your happiness!

Gather with Friends or Family
When you are around people you enjoy, you will be happier! So it looks like it's an excellent time for a party or even a lunch date.

Que up Your Playlist
Listening to your favorite songs will put you in a happy mood!

Carpe Diem!
Seize the day, grab the bull by the horns, and live with no regrets! Living your life the way you want to live is crucial to your happiness.

Ommmm

Even for a short time, meditation will connect you to your higher self and make you happier! So don't worry about how your meditation session goes. Even a little meditation is so much better than none.

Just Laugh Through It

Finding humor in less-than-ideal situations will make you a happier person.

Have Fun!

Having fun should go without saying, but having fun, on your terms, is where the happy lives!

No Comparison

You are such a unique and wonderful person! Stop comparing yourself to others and instead focus on the extraordinary qualities about yourself - there are tons of them!

TV? What TV?

Reducing TV (or screen time in general) by 50% will make you happier! Think of all the wonderful things you can fill that time. Seriously. Think about them and make a list!

Seven Minutes

Seven minutes of exercise is all it takes to create more happiness in your life. Even walking laps around your living room will even do the trick. Just keep going for 7 minutes!

Green Thumb

Having house plants will make you happier! Seeing them and caring for them gives you pride and accomplishment. We can all use extra boosts of those.

5+ a Day
The more fruits and veggies you eat, the happier you will be! All of those colors do your body good, and when your body is happy, you are happy.

Get Outta Here
Declutter your space! Too much stuff takes up space in your brain. Letting go of material things you don't need allows you to let go of mental things you don't need either.

Make it About YOU
What makes one person happy may not make *you* happy, so make it a priority to check in with yourself to ensure you are doing things that make *you* happy!

Get Your Freak On
Having sex once a week will make you happier! Don't have a partner? No worries. Solo sex works just as well. ;)

Hello?
Calling somebody instead of texting them puts an extra pep in your step. We all need that human interaction!

Animals
Spending time with your pets or somebody else's will make you happier!

ZZZzzzzz
Make sure you get enough sleep! Being sleepy makes us crabby, and that's the opposite of where we want to be.

Free Yourself

Claiming your freedom, whatever that looks like to you, will make you happier than any amount of money ever will. So, where do you feel tied down?

Nurture Your Relationships

Feeling good about your relationships will make you happier than $100,000! (Hmmm. Notice the trend here?) What can you do to nurture a relationship right now?

Fake Yourself Out

If you aren't feeling happy, fake it! Soon real happiness will take over, and you won't be faking anymore!

Color Explosion!

Yellow, and other bright colors, increase your happiness! Take a look at the colors around your home and your wardrobe. Are they doing their part in your happiness?

Choose It!

It should go without saying but we need to make our happiness a choice. Choose to be happy. Some days it may be easier than others, and that's okay. Watch your thoughts and how you feel. If you aren't feeling as happy as you'd like, do something to make you feel happier!

Find Some Water!

Being outside by water will make you happier! (It's because of all of those negative ions!) It can be the ocean, a lake, a pond, or even a fountain. If the weather is warm, you'll get bonus happy points.

Go Outside

Being in nature simply makes us happier. Twenty minutes is your goal, but any amount of time will help. What can you do outside that you usually do inside? It's time to make the switch and do those things outside!

Community

Being a *part* of something bigger than yourself will make you happier. It could be the town you live in or even something small like a group of like-minded people. Simply get involved in something for your happiness.

Remember When?

Thinking about happy memories will make you happy in the present! So tell somebody about those memories and laugh, laugh, laugh!

Challenge Bound

Challenging yourself with a doable task will make you happier because you will have achieved something.

Hug it Out

Hugging makes you happier because it releases oxytocin - the feel-good hormone! Who can you enjoy a hug with right now? If there's nobody around you that you want to hug, hugging yourself works just as well.

Talk About It

Speaking about a problem you have will help you resolve it quickly and make you feel happier because it will help to release your burden surrounding the issue. You can talk to a therapist, a friend, or even out loud to yourself!

How Ya Walkin'?

Take stock if you're walking as tall as you can be. When you walk tall, it increases your confidence and makes you happier!

How I Love Thee

Write down all the things you love about yourself! Don't be shy - list all the reasons you think you are great!

Dance Like You Mean It

Dance around your house to your favorite songs! Get dramatic, be silly, and show your sexy. Freeing yourself to dance will shoot your happiness through the roof!

Go Ahead. Try It!

Trying new things will make you happier because it will force you to think differently and use your brain differently. It'll shake things up, and you'll feel happier!

I'm So Grateful

Starting a gratitude list is sure to make you a happier person. You will be looking for things to be grateful for, and you will also let the powers that be know exactly what you love! Of course, if you make this a daily habit, that's even better.

Color Me Happy

Coloring will make your heart sing! Coloring will calm your brain's fear center and has the same calming effects as meditation.

Let the Light Shine

The lighter and brighter your room is, the happier you will be! It increases not only your happiness but your motivation.

Get Dirty

Somehow, someway, get your hands dirty today! Something like finger painting will work, but ideally, you'll get your hands in some dirt today. Getting dirty leads to happiness, and getting in actual dirt has grounding properties for your body!

Oh, the places you'll see!

Make a list of ALL the places you want to travel to! You'll get even more happiness for your effort if you write a short sentence or two about why you want to go and what you want to see there!

Thank Someone

Send a thank-you note through the mail or even an email or text. Thank the person for something they did. It will make you feel happy to know you've made somebody else happy!

Go on a news diet.

It's time to turn off the news! If you feel it's essential to stay in the know, find a source online or an informed friend to get the vital info from. Otherwise, stay away from the news so you feel happier!

Happiness Multiplied

Since you want to be happier, do more things that make you happy! The more you pursue happiness, the quicker it will become a habit.

Compliments!

Hand out compliments like they are a dime a dozen! Actually, they are better than that because they are free to give, and they make somebody feel like a million bucks. Plus, of course, making others feel good helps *you* feel good.

Life isn't always perfect.

Accept the fact that life is unpredictable! It can get messy, and things you don't like can happen. So just accept those times for what they are and get on with doing more things that make you happy.

The Release Valve

Get out your journal and write away your frustrations! Then, when you get them *out* of your mind and give them to paper, you can release them and feel so much better.

Spend with consciousness.

Where we spend our money can make us feel really happy! Find out what businesses support and then choose to spend your money at places that match your beliefs. Also, give to nonprofits that support the things important to you in life.

Meditate

You don't need to become the next meditation expert. Just fit in 3 minutes of meditation each day. If your passion grows, follow it; but you can gain a lot with a mere 3 minutes.

Get Excited!

Always have something that you're looking forward to! A vacation, a project, or something as simple as a great cup of tea at night. The more you look forward to it, the more excitement you'll create in your life, and when we're excited, we're happy!

Smile, please!

Smiling is something that we can do to fake it until we make it. Make it a genuine smile, though, and get your eyes involved. Ideally, you'll be smiling because you mean it; but even if you have to fake it, it'll help you get happier.

Hey, You're Good!

Spend more time doing things you are good at doing! It will make you feel good to do them, which creates all kinds of good feelings, equating to more happiness!

Wander Outside

Getting outside is *so* good for you! The dirt, the sunshine, and the negative ions all do such beautiful things for your mood and happiness overall.

Plan that trip.

Plan a trip you dream of - even if you never go! Find all the great places you want to see, the cuisine you want to eat, the places you want to sleep, and more! Don't forget your travel accommodations to get there and when you *are* there (how you will get around). Planning for a trip creates happiness!

Play Catch!

Grab a friend, or even just throw a ball around in the air by yourself! Playing with a ball brings back childhood innocence and makes us happy! (Not to mention the exercise you'll get!)

Read a GOOD Book

Get a book that you are *excited* to read! Books take us places, and it doesn't matter if it's fiction or non-fiction. Just find one that you are stoked to read.

Movie Time!
Watch one of your favorite movies! It'll make you feel good.

Get Out
Outside that is. Go outside and appreciate the blue sky, the clouds, the sun, and the breeze on your face. Relish in its magnificence, and you will go back inside feeling a deep appreciation and increased happiness.

Declutter!
Getting rid of things you no longer need frees up space in your mind and allows more happiness into your life: declutter your entire home, or even just a room or a drawer.

Be good to you.
Do something special for yourself. Buy that small trinket, light a candle, or take the time to write in your journal or slip into a nice hot bubble bath. Even the smallest amount of self-pampering will increase your happiness!

Grab that pen and paper!
Write an actual letter to somebody! Let them know how much you appreciate them and why. Let them know what's going on in your life and why it makes you happy — simply touching base with them in a handwritten letter will make you both happy!

Clean!
A clean home helps to clean your thinking as well. Cleaning is a mindful activity, and it also frees up space in your head for more productive thoughts. A clean home is a happy mind! If you don't want to clean your entire home, just pick one room or space!

Garden

Plant some food or flowers! Getting your hands in the dirt is an excellent way to release negativity in your life. Plus, caring for what you planted and reaping the rewards makes for a happy you!

Good Music

Listen to some music that makes you feel good! Happiness comes from simply hearing it, but it makes you feel even better if you add in singing or dancing!

Self Care

Take care of yourself. That may look like creating a system to take care of your money or giving yourself a pedicure. But, whatever taking care of you *means to you,* do it! It will make you feel so good to have it done.

Be Grateful

Start a gratitude journal and write down five things you're grateful for daily. The more we acknowledge how grateful we are, the more experiences we'll have that make us even *more* grateful.

Join a Club

Find a club that focuses on something you enjoy! You will create more time for your pleasures and meet people you can talk to and learn from. Happiness abounds!

Get some culture!

Go to a museum or a local play! Either of those will expand your thinking and create new experiences in your life, which means more happiness for you.

Set A Goal

Set a specific, highly attainable goal. The kind of goal where there is no question you will achieve it when you put effort towards it. The work you put in and the attainment of the goal will make you so happy! (Set a new goal after you finish this one!)

Let Go

It might be time to let go of some outdated beliefs and dreams. (DON'T let go of a dream because you don't think it can come true! ONLY let go of a dream if you fully realize you simply don't want it anymore!) Think about your closest held beliefs and dreams. Do they still hold true for you? Could you question them and see if you're ready for something new? Letting go of what you genuinely don't want creates freedom and happiness in your life!

All the Good

Write down at least three good things that happened today. Like being grateful, when you acknowledge good things that happened to you, you will draw more of those good things into your life! Plus, it will keep you on the lookout for good things throughout your day. You're likely to see more good when you look for the good!

Visualize

Visualize you living the life you dream of and see it as already happening! When you end your visualization, tell yourself, "All this or something better." If you can see it in your mind, you can see it in your life. (This is best when done every day!)

Act As If

Acting *as if* is like taking visualization and living it in your everyday life. Get in the mindset that you already ARE that famous artist, that you ARE a thriving entrepreneur, that you ARE precisely what you want to be. Walk around *knowing* you are living that life. It will add a special pep to your step. You'll make different decisions that you otherwise would have, and you will be so happy!

Be Present

Make an effort to be present in what you're doing and who you're talking to. Fully submerge yourself in the situation without thinking other thoughts (and not being on your phone!) Being present will allow you to live your life to the fullest and find happiness!

Make A List

Make a list of your favorite things that make you feel good! Maybe it's a specific tea or coffee, stretch, or activity that makes you feel good and happy. Refer to this list when you need a quick reminder of something that will make you happy. (This book is a great alternative, and it *is* the purpose of this book! Dog-ear the pages, put sticky notes on your favorite pages, or star the things you like most.)

Do what you are drawn to do.

What gives you a sense of purpose, or what is it that when you're done doing, you feel accomplished? Do more of that thing! It certainly will bring happiness into your life!

Acceptance

Accept a situation for what it is. If something is going on that you don't like, you can either do something about it, support those actively doing something about it, or let it go. Do what feels best, and you will make more room for happiness.

Who do you want to be?

Make a list of the qualities you want to embody, how you want to develop, what skills you want to learn, etc. Then, take even small steps each day to become that person. Being who you most want to be will create a *ton* of happiness in your life!

Unleash Your Creativity!

We all are creative beings. So do something that allows your creativity to come out and play! If you don't know what that is, just try something new. Creativity allows our happiness to soar!

Down Time

Take time to relax and *enjoy* your relaxation! Everybody has time to relax for five minutes, so take that 5 minutes and enjoy your time. Of course, the more time, the better! Put you first. You deserve it!

Clean Sheets

Who doesn't love the feel of slipping into a clean, crisp bed at night?! Wash your sheets and your blankets (if you can)! It will make you happy falling asleep and what we feel when we go to sleep is likely the mood we will wake up feeling!

Step out of your comfort zone.

Stepping out of your comfort zone doesn't need to be something huge! It can be as small as parting your hair on the opposite side or deciding to dance around your home all day instead of walking. But, of course, if you want to do something big, go for it! Any amount of activity out of your comfort zone will stir new thoughts and bring new confidence!

Party Time!

Plan a party! If you don't end up throwing the party, no harm is done; but just the act of *planning* raises your endorphins and puts good images in your head (which makes us happy!) What is the party for? Who is invited? Live band or DJ? Who will cater the food? Where will it be? Have fun and plan a full-out bash!

What you really want.

Write about what you *really* want your reality to look like. For example, do you want to have great luck all the time, feel magical because your every wish comes true, and be surrounded by loving, like-minded people? Write it down! Pretend it is actually happening! The more you do this, the better it will be because you will draw these experiences into your life, making you over the moon happy!

NOTES, THOUGHTS & IDEAS

_____
_____
_____
_____
_____
_____
_____
_____
_____
_____
_____
_____
_____
_____
_____
_____
_____
_____
_____
_____
_____
_____

NOTES, THOUGHTS & IDEAS

_____
_____
_____
_____
_____
_____
_____
_____
_____
_____
_____
_____
_____
_____
_____
_____
_____
_____
_____
_____
_____

Do for Others

Doing for yourself is always encouraged, but doing things for others will put you on the fast track to happiness! Because of that, there's a whole list of ideas about what you can do for others.

Smile!
Smiling at somebody may be precisely what they need to improve their day! You can smile and fill it with love and acceptance, or if you're feelin' saucy, smile like you just did something on the mischievous side! Either way, it will help make someone's day.

Send A Card
Pick out a card to send to somebody out of the blue. It will catch them off guard and make their day!

Check On Somebody
Call somebody just to see how they are doing, making the conversation all about *them* by asking questions or just allowing them to vent if they need to.

Indulge Your Pets

Sometimes our pets "get in our way at the most inconvenient times." When they do, take the time to give them what they need! Petting them, love, or playtime - whatever it is, give it freely to them.

Pick Some Flowers

Pick some flowers in your yard or some wildflowers and give them to somebody for no reason!

Feed Their Tummy

Go out of your way to make somebody their favorite meal! It will make them feel so special and loved.

Do Their Chores

Chores are, well, a chore. So take somebody's chore off their plate for the day. It will be a real treat for them! (This can also flow over into doing their errands for the day!)

How I Love Thee

Write a letter of love or admiration to somebody! It doesn't need to be a long letter, but it can be. Let them know precisely why you love or admire them.

Give A Book

Give somebody a book you love! Put a little note inside the book telling them why *you* enjoy the book and why you think they would love it too.

Bake!

Bake somebody cookies, a cake, or brownies! Everybody loves a special treat now and then. If you know they have dietary limitations, include the recipe so they know it's safe for them to eat!

Praise

Spread the good about somebody by praising them to somebody else! The person you're praising can be present or not - it doesn't matter. Just talk good about them!

Show Appreciation

Thank somebody for something they did. Maybe they held the door for you or did something huge for you! Just say thank you and make sure they know you mean it!

Be Aware And Help

Pay attention to what is going on in a friend or loved one's life and let them know you are available if they need you. You can tell when somebody is going through a hard time or had a bad day, so offer up a listening ear or ask them what you can do for them. Don't take a polite no for an answer. Help them.

HUG!

Hug somebody that you usually wouldn't hug or hug somebody extra good! Hugging does so much good, especially when it's heart to heart.

Have Fun!

Take somebody out on a friend date! Plan activities around what *they* enjoy and allow yourself to enjoy the experience too.

I Love You

Many times we take love for granted. Let somebody know you love them by *telling* them, "I love you!"

I'm Proud Of You

Most people are working toward a goal or have just achieved something big. Tell them that you are proud of them and why! It will boost their confidence!

Help Them Achieve

Help somebody achieve a goal! You can brainstorm with them, teach them something or connect them with somebody who can help them. Any of those will show your support for them.

Just Because

Buy or make somebody a thoughtful gift *just because*. No reason is needed except for the recipient to be happy.

Care Package

Put together a special care package for somebody and give it to them! Think about *their* likes and dislikes while putting it together, but there is nothing wrong with introducing them to something *you* like as well. Make sure to include a little note about why they deserve this package!

List Their Goodness

Make a list of things you admire and love about somebody! Everybody deserves to have this kind of list given to them because it gives them insight that they may not recognize about themselves.

Secret Admirer

Leave nice notes for somebody to find, telling them why they are fantastic! Don't add your name, though - it makes it more intriguing for them!

Support Our Feathered Friends

Put out a simple bird feeder and birdbath! Your generosity will be rewarded by being able to watch them enjoy it.

Tip Big!

The next time you are given the opportunity to tip - tip extra big! The person receiving it will be *so* happy!

A Sincere Hello

When you pass a stranger, make eye contact with them, smile, and say hello! You might be the catalyst for an excellent day for that person.

Mind Your Manners

Say please and thank you! It is often overlooked anymore, and you'll catch somebody off guard when you say it to them. (In a good way!)

Say Their Name

Make sure to use somebody's name when you talk to them. Our name is our favorite word, and when we hear it, we perk up and pay more attention. This goes for the people we usually call "Honey" to the service rep we talk to on the phone.

Kind Driver

Be nice while driving and let somebody in front of you or allow them to make their move - whatever crazy move they may make. It's not worth getting upset while driving and your kindness could be repaid as a happy chain reaction between others.

Be A Good Neighbor

Do something nice for your neighbor! For example, take them a small gift or even just wave hello!

Acknowledge Hard Work

Keep your mail carrier, sanitary worker, housekeeper, etc., in good spirits by giving them a small gift or a tip! They work hard and are hardly acknowledged for their committed efforts.

Say You're Sorry

If you've messed up, own up to it and apologize. We often make excuses for what we did, but a sincere "I'm sorry" goes a long way if the other person feels slighted.

Homemade Gift

Give someone a homemade gift that *you* made! Make anything you want; even if you're *not* good at it. The friendly intention is behind the giving. It makes somebody feel special knowing that you spent time and effort on them.

An Old Thank You

Think back on your past and reach out to somebody who helped you somehow. It is such a special gift that you can give. They will know you appreciate them *and* have remembered it all these years.

Special Recipe

Write down your favorite recipe you've created and give it to your friends! They will be able to make and enjoy your creation, and they will also think of you every time they make it.

Bee Kind To Wildlife

Create a garden for bees and butterflies! Bees are so important to our environment, and butterflies are a delight to watch.

"You yourself, as much as anybody in the entire universe, deserve your love and affection."
~ Buddha

NOTES, THOUGHTS & IDEAS

_____
_____
_____
_____
_____
_____
_____
_____
_____
_____
_____
_____
_____
_____
_____
_____
_____
_____
_____
_____
_____

HAPPINESS FACT
Watching funny videos, TV shows or movies will make you happier!

Self Love Boosters

Loving yourself is imperative to a happy life! You deserve to be #1 in your own life, no doubt about it.

In this section, you will find a simple list of ways to show yourself love.

Number One
Make yourself your number one priority! Seriously.

Say No!
You don't have to do something if you don't want to.

Say Yes!
If you *want* to do something - give that gift to yourself!

Forgive Yourself And Others
Forgiveness is for yourself, not for the other person. So allow the mistakes of others *and the mistakes you've made*, and forgive. We all do as well as we can at the moment we do it.

Dear Future Me
Write a letter to your future self! Talk about the excitement you have for the future, and show gratitude to yourself for making it happen!

Flowers

Buy yourself some flowers. You deserve them!

Thank You

Accept a compliment graciously! You're receiving it for a reason, so own up to the fact that you are fantastic and deserve it!

Meditate

Even if for a short time, sit quietly while focusing on your breath. When you are present (which is what meditation does), you are the closest to your higher self. You deserve that and owe it to yourself to get to know her (your higher self).

Pete And Repeat

Repeat to yourself, "I love and accept myself!" Repeat it when you're busy doing other things, and repeat it to yourself when you have time to focus on the meaning behind the words. *Feel them true!*

Can I Have A Hug?

Ask for a hug if you want one! It is excellent for you *and* makes the other person feel like they are helping you.

Allow Your Curiosity

Pursue and explore your passions and desires! We are here to live and enjoy! Do what you love!!!

Sing!

Singing and humming activate your throat chakra and make it easier to express your true self! We're not much happier than when we are our true selves, so sing loud and proud!

Organize Your Money

Getting your finances in order may not seem like a fun time to many people, but having it done puts you in a state of knowing, and that *knowing* is freeing.

Worry No More

When we worry, we are putting our thoughts on the future. It's *your* future, so you can make anything happen. When you worry, think about the worst and best-case scenarios and let it go by getting in the present moment. Pay attention to your breath. Name every object that you see. Do something productive while repeating a good, positive affirmation.

Watch Your Words!

Complaining is a part of our culture. It's time to stop that! We speak the words we believe and the thoughts we think. Since what we think becomes the truth in our lives, it's imperative to watch those words and thoughts! You seriously owe yourself *good* thoughts and words.

Joyful Movement

What kind of physical movement feels good to you? A walk, dancing, lifting weights, doing the crab walk?! When we move our bodies, we move our energy, and energy in motion stays in motion. *But*, of course, enjoy the movement!

Surround Yourself with Positivity

We are the company we keep, so surround yourself with positive people, images, words, and an overall positive environment! If you need to, join a special club or book club where you and your positive efforts will be supported.

Treat Yourself

Get yourself a gift! It's even better if it's something meaningful that reminds you of your journey toward fulfillment.

Use The Guest Towels

Use and enjoy all the "special" things you have! Your nice silverware, plates, towels, soaps, perfume, anything that you save for a special reason - use it with abandon! *You* being *you* is special enough!

YES!

Write encouraging affirmations or notes and leave them on your mirror! Then, when you see them, look into your eyes and say them to yourself.

Get Out

Go outside and enjoy Mother Nature! Even if it's for 5 minutes. Enjoy the season and soak it up. Nature has a way of taking your problems and leaving you happy.

Ask For Help

Contrary to what we are taught by society, we simply do *not* have to do it all. Instead, ask for help when you need it and accept help when somebody offers.

Feel Good Clothes

Wear clothes that make you feel good! Maybe it's a fancy dress and heels, or leggings and a sweatshirt. If it makes you feel good, wear it!

Drink Up!

Water is so vital to our bodies and our mood! So make sure you drink plenty of water! You can add something special by doing the Magic Recipe called "Charge It Up!"

Take A Class

Get out of your comfort zone or get out of a rut by taking a class and learning something new! All kinds of websites offer classes, or you can get out to the community college or find a community class. It will shake up your energy and create new opportunities for you!

The Cooking Mood

Set the mood while cooking by lighting some candles, listening to good music, and channeling your inner Betty Crocker. It makes mealtime much more meaningful!

Phone Be Done!

Turn off that phone. It sucks our energy and our time. If you can't turn it off, leave it somewhere you won't just naturally grab it and zone out. Instead, have a good book, take care of your to-do list, or simply *live*!

I Love Me

Practice loving yourself without judgment. You are *exactly* where you are supposed to be right now! Love yourself for being you. If you're having trouble, pick one thing you love about yourself and dwell on that. Your list will begin to grow.

Clean/Organize/Declutter

When our homes and spaces are unkempt, we tend to continually put things off that are important because the chaos around us takes our energy. So tidy up your space and free your mind!

I Did That

Make a list of all of your big and small accomplishments! Keep this list handy to keep filling out because you will amaze yourself by remembering so many things! Plus, this ever-growing list is quite a confidence booster!

Mindful Meals

Be mindful when you eat. No phones. No TV. No computers. Just you and your food. Enjoy it. Savor it. Be grateful for how it is nourishing your body.

Fun Ahead!

Make a list of all the fun things you want to do in the next three months! Then, you can take it a step further and buy tickets you may need, book a room for an overnight stay, or get those new hiking boots! But your fun activities don't need to be extreme. Perhaps your kind of fun is completing a book series or repainting your house! Just make sure it is fun for *you*!

Dear Past Me

Write a letter to your past self to congratulate yourself for making it no matter the odds and forgive yourself for things you might have done wrong. We know more now than we did then. So it's time to let yourself off the hook for past mistakes and celebrate your victories!

Be Kind To You

Sometimes we do things that aren't that fun, like eating a salad instead of a burger. When you do those things, say to yourself, "I am choosing this for my body because I love her!" (Your higher, *true* self.)

You Are Unique

We tend to compare ourselves to others. Stop doing that! You are such a unique and wonderful being! If you were any less *you*, you wouldn't be giving your best to yourself and to the world. No more comparisons. Only celebrations of you.

Trust Yourself

You are a brilliant and intuitive person! Trust yourself in any given situation and show yourself that respect.

Mirror Speak

Give yourself a good ol' pep talk in the mirror. Talk to yourself like you would talk to your child or best friend. You are amazing, and you should tell yourself!

Introducing... ME!

Write an introduction that somebody would give for you. Talk about the great things you've accomplished and why you are the perfect person for whatever the introduction is for. You can even do this as if it is your *future* self! Make the introduction based on the person you are becoming!

Solo Vacation

Plan a vacation that you will take by yourself! You don't *have* to actually take it - planning it is enough, but why not go through with it?! Decide where you'll go, what you want to see and do, where you'll stay, everything! It's all about you, so it'll be perfect!

Celebrate!

There is always a reason to celebrate! Throw a party or just have a memorable time with yourself.

How Else?

Ask yourself, "How else can I look at this?" It will help you develop different solutions or a better way of looking at something. You can do this in *any* area of your life!

To-Do

Do the one thing on your to-do list that always gets pushed aside. It will feel so good to have it done!

Friend Audit

Take a look at your friends, acquaintances, and even your family. If anybody makes you feel bad about yourself or drains you, either cut them out of your life or dramatically reduce the time you spend with them. We don't have time for bad friends!

Life Motto

Create a life motto for yourself! Think of what is very important to you and make it a rule you live by. It feels good, and it can help guide your decisions. If something fits in with your motto - do it! If it *doesn't* fit - don't do it.

Dream Big

Dreams are meant to be BIG! So many people are afraid to want something so big and then fail. But instead of looking at it like that, look at it as if it just hasn't happened yet. Plus, so many people do great big things with their lives! *Why can't that be you?*

Be YOU

Being yourself is *absolutely* vital to your happiness. Be you, be *proud* to be you, and let that weirdness shine! We are all *so* unique, and the world deserves to see you at your best!

NOTES, THOUGHTS & IDEAS

_____
_____
_____
_____
_____
_____
_____
_____
_____
_____
_____
_____
_____
_____
_____
_____
_____
_____
_____
_____
_____
_____
_____
_____

HAPPINESS FACT
The more fruits & veggies you eat,
the happier you are!

NOTES, THOUGHTS & IDEAS

_____
_____
_____
_____
_____
_____
_____
_____
_____
_____
_____
_____
_____
_____
_____
_____
_____
_____
_____
_____

Section 2 — Convey Your Desires

Part of being happy is seeing all of your desires come to fruition in your life. In this section, you will read about how you can convey your personal desires directly to your mind and to spirit - putting you on the fast path to success.

Visualizations

Visualizing is an excellent way to practice your future life and find excitement about how wonderful your life is becoming.

These are made-for-you visualizations to put yourself front and center in the life you are going for! You can simply read these aloud while seeing the imagery in your mind or record them on your phone to settle in and allow the images to unfold in your mind as you listen to your recording. A perk to recording these visualizations on your own is that you can tweak anything that you'd like to change.

While doing visualizations, it is normal to have confusing language patterns. It helps to confuse your thinking mind a little bit so you can more easily slide into a relaxed state.

If you go to ErinChavez.com/FGTHBonus, these visualizations are pre-recorded and available as a free download!

Affirmations

Holy cow, you have a lot of affirmations to choose from! You can pick one a day, once a week, once a month, one an hour... whatever feels good to you! After choosing your affirmation, put it on your mirror, on the fridge, on your computer monitor, as your phone wallpaper, in your car, or wherever you will see it regularly. The key to affirmations is to get so comfortable with them that they become second nature to you. You'll see them and think, "Of course!" So say them, write them, or listen to them on repeat.

Affirmations are repeated so you can create new pathways in your brain. Repeating affirmations literally rewires your brain to achieve what the affirmation states.

It is crucial to have affirmations because we all have negative thoughts, beliefs, and programming in different areas of our lives. It's time to boot out the bad and install the new ones! Remember, your reality is what you make it, so these affirmations are essential!

NOTES, THOUGHTS & IDEAS

_____
_____
_____
_____
_____
_____
_____
_____
_____
_____
_____
_____
_____
_____
_____
_____
_____
_____
_____
_____
_____

NOTES, THOUGHTS & IDEAS

_____
_____
_____
_____
_____
_____
_____
_____
_____
_____
_____
_____
_____
_____
_____
_____
_____
_____
_____
_____

Visualizations

These visualizations are made for you to put yourself front and center in the life you are going for! You can simply read these aloud while seeing the imagery in your mind or record them on your phone to settle in and allow the images to unfold in your mind as you listen to your recording. A perk to recording these visualizations on your own is that you can tweak anything that you'd like to change.

You will notice the beginnings and endings of each visualization are the same. That is so you can get used to hearing and doing them, so they work more effectively.

Tips for Recording

When you see the visualizations, you will notice *(italicized words and parentheses)*. That is to indicate directions for you when reading or recording the visualizations for yourself. Don't record that portion of the visualization, just pause that amount of time, or follow the direction given before you continue recording. If there are no directions between lines, just take a short pause before reading the following line. While recording, you will want to read much slower and calmer than you usually speak.

If you go to ErinChavez.com/FGTHBonus, these visualizations are pre-recorded and available as a free download!

Finding Happiness
Visualization

Welcome to your visualization. You deserve this time to create the life you want for yourself.

As you settle into a position that is comfortable for you, start to notice your breath.

(pause 15 seconds)

There is no need to control it or make it slower. In fact, you may notice that simply by *noticing* your breath, it will begin to slow, and perhaps it will deepen as well.

(pause 5 seconds)

Just keep noticing your breath...

(pause 5 seconds)

When a thought comes to your mind, notice that it is there, release it, and go back to your breath.

(pause 20 seconds)

Now, as you breathe in, imagine a beautiful glow of the color you choose, being inhaled and filling your entire body.

(pause 10 seconds)

As you exhale, release any negativity you may have built up inside of you. Your exhales are a great time to make sure your body is all relaxed, and you release any tensions in your muscles.

(pause 10 seconds)

Remember, with each inhale, you are growing the beautiful glow... it fills your body so much it starts to surround your body and maybe even fill the room you're in right now.

(pause 20 seconds)

This glow is the glow of pure love. You have pure love filling your body and surrounding your body.

Keep breathing. Keep noticing the beautiful, growing glow. Keep releasing any negativity and tensions.

The next time you hear my voice, we will begin the visualization process to create the life you want...

(pause 30 seconds)

**

We are about to design the type of happiness that feels good to you. But, of course, happiness doesn't look the same to everybody, so it is okay to go down a path that may appear different from what most people want.

Conjure up an image of someplace that brings about feelings of happiness for you.

It can be in the past... the present... or even in the future.

(pause 5 seconds)

Just as long as you feel that happiness.

(pause 15 seconds)

Now it's time to really fill out this image in your mind. If you can, include visual clues and anything you hear, what you can touch, aromas, and maybe even special foods. There might be pictures on the walls that show a great vacation, your perfect house, or something else. Maybe there are huge windows that overlook your perfect scenery... Take a few moments to allow this image to really develop.

(pause 30 seconds)

You are surrounded by happiness. Look around and find something that really makes you happy. Walk over to it and really appreciate it for what it is. Allow the gratitude for it to grow.

(pause 20 seconds)

Now, look around again and find something else. Walk over to *it* and appreciate it for everything it means to you - all the happiness it gives.

(pause 20 seconds)

And one more time... look around and find something else that really makes you happy. Walk to it and really take it in... feel the happiness it gives and allow the gratitude you have for it to fill you.

(pause 20 seconds)

Recall the three things you just picked that made you so very happy and filled you with gratitude.

Imagine each of them fitting in its own glass orb. Lay all three glass orbs out in front of you. Allow yourself to get in a comfortable position to really witness these things that make you happy.

(pause 15 seconds)

While looking at these three things that make you happy, what is the underlying reason each one of them brings you happiness? It might be because they evoke feelings of love, pleasure, excitement, achievement, or something else. It's okay if what is enclosed in each orb brings up a different feeling.

Take a few moments and decide what feeling each item gives you.

(pause 25 seconds)

You now have at least one feeling that you *know* brings you happiness. You *may* have three feelings that bring you happiness.

Now, imagine yourself somewhere you find tranquil. It doesn't matter where it is, as long as you feel peaceful being there. Take just a moment to find that place for you.

(pause 15 seconds)

As you are in your tranquil place, recall the feeling or feelings that you know brings you happiness.

(pause 5 seconds)

Think about how you can incorporate those feelings into your daily life. What can you do that will bring about those feelings? Consider that for a moment.

(pause 30 seconds)

Decide that you will pursue those things that you just came up with. It can be in big or small ways but promise yourself you will fit those things into your daily life. Doing so will bring about so much happiness in your life.

**

(quicken your voice and allow it to sound more upbeat and normal)

You've done a very good job today! You have successfully established what your life is. A life filled with love, happiness, and all the wonderful things love and happiness holds for you.

It's time to start to wiggle your toes... your fingers... start to move your body a little bit...

When you are ready, you can open your eyes.

Money Flows to Me Visualization

Welcome to your visualization. You deserve this time to create the life you want for yourself.

As you settle into a position that is comfortable for you, start to notice your breath.

(pause 15 seconds)

There is no need to control it or make it slower. In fact, you may notice that simply by *noticing* your breath, it will begin to slow, and perhaps it will deepen as well.

(pause 5 seconds)

Just keep noticing your breath...

(pause 5 seconds)

When a thought comes to your mind, notice that it is there, release it, and go back to your breath.

(pause 20 seconds)

Now, as you breathe in, imagine a beautiful glow of the color you choose, being inhaled and filling your entire body.

(pause 10 seconds)

As you exhale, release any negativity you may have built up inside of you. Your exhales are a great time to make sure your body is all relaxed, and you release any tensions in your muscles.

(pause 10 seconds)

118

Remember, with each inhale, you are growing the beautiful glow... it fills your body so much it starts to surround your body and maybe even fill the room you're in right now.

(pause 20 seconds)

This glow is the glow of pure love. You have pure love filling your body and surrounding your body.

Keep breathing. Keep noticing the beautiful, growing glow. Keep releasing any negativity and tensions.

The next time you hear my voice, we will begin the visualization process to create the life you want...

(pause 30 seconds)

**

Imagine yourself sitting someplace safe where things are *flowing* next to you. It could be a river, a creek, the beach, outer space, on the top of a windy hill... Anywhere you can imagine *something* flowing past you.

(pause 10 seconds)

Is it sunny or dark? Are other people nearby, or are you alone? What kind of comfortable clothing are you wearing? Are there any distinct smells, sounds, or physical feelings? Take a moment and let that image develop fully in your mind.

(pause 20 seconds)

As you are sitting there, you suddenly notice something flowing past you. You find it curious, but you keep developing this image in your mind.

(pause 10 seconds)

Again... something just went flowing past you, but there were 3, maybe four different things this time! You decide to pay attention and see what is happening.

Sure enough, you see about ten more things coming toward you! You try to grab them as they flow by and notice it's money! There are checks, cash, digital encryptions...! All kinds of money are flowing by you!

The more you look, the more money you see! It's everywhere, all around you, flowing, flowing, flowing...

Now that you are aware that money is always coming, and the more you pay attention, the more money there is, you decide you're going to grab some!

You pull out something that will catch the money.

(pause 5 seconds)

As you start accumulating all of this money, you realize there is *way* more money than you would ever need! At first, you think you should get every last bit that is possible, but as you continue seeing all of this money flowing by, you realize it's always going to be there. You just need to open your eyes to it to see all the money.

You realize there is so much money out there that there is enough for everybody in the world and that it's available anytime you want some.

You go somewhere where you can take your attention off the flow of money all around you. You count what you just accumulated, and WOW, it's enough for everything you want!

Take a moment to think about everything you will do and buy with the money you just accumulated.

(pause 20 seconds)

There is nothing too small or too big. Nothing is greedy; you deserve anything and everything you want!

You realized that you actually have *more* money than you need right now, and you want to give some away. For a moment, think about who you want to give it to, and imagine the surprise on their face and the pure happiness you'll feel in your heart.

(pause 20 seconds)

What a great day you've spent accumulating all of this money! You decide that you have plenty of money for now because you know that at any time you want more money, all you need to do is to realize it is flowing by you - all of the time, money is flowing into your life. It flows to you faster than you can spend it.

And remember - this flow of money is available to everyone! You simply cannot take more than your fair share because money is abundant and flows all around. You can return to the flow of money wherever you'd like.

**

(quicken your voice and allow it to sound more upbeat and normal)

You've done a very good job today! You have successfully established what your life is. A life filled with love, happiness, and all the wonderful things love and happiness holds for you.

It's time to start to wiggle your toes... your fingers... start to move your body a little bit...

When you are ready, you can open your eyes.

Free to be Me
Visualization

Welcome to your visualization. You deserve this time to create the life you want for yourself.

As you settle into a position that is comfortable for you, start to notice your breath.

(pause 15 seconds)

There is no need to control it or make it slower. In fact, you may notice that simply by *noticing* your breath, it will begin to slow, and perhaps it will deepen as well.

(pause 5 seconds)

Just keep noticing your breath...

(pause 5 seconds)

When a thought comes to your mind, notice that it is there, release it, and go back to your breath.

(pause 20 seconds)

Now, as you breathe in, imagine a beautiful glow of the color you choose, being inhaled and filling your entire body.

(pause 10 seconds)

As you exhale, release any negativity you may have built up inside of you. Your exhales are a great time to make sure your body is all relaxed, and you release any tensions in your muscles.

(pause 10 seconds)

Remember, with each inhale, you are growing the beautiful glow... it fills your body so much it starts to surround your body and maybe even fill the room you're in right now.

(pause 20 seconds)

This glow is the glow of pure love. You have pure love filling your body and surrounding your body.

Keep breathing. Keep noticing the beautiful, growing glow. Keep releasing any negativity and tensions.

The next time you hear my voice, we will begin the visualization process to create the life you want...

(pause 30 seconds)

**

You are in a safe place to explore who you *truly* want to be. You are *always* free to be yourself; you only need to permit yourself to let that happen.

Imagine yourself sitting in a comfortable room filled with loving energy. You see yourself sitting in the corner of this room filled with love. You recognize that you feel hidden, cocooned by who people *think* you are, not who you *really* are. This may even include you, *yourself*, hiding your true self.

(pause 10 seconds)

It is time to break free from these restraints.

First, take a moment to acknowledge there is *nobody* who can keep you trapped. It is only *you* who can keep you hidden away in this corner.

Second, realize that if somebody has an issue with who you truly are, they are not for you. You deserve to be surrounded by people who love and adore the *real* you!

Imagine you getting up from the corner in this room and shaking free of fear. You shake your feet, legs, arms, and hands to release anything that has been holding you down.

(pause 10 seconds)

You walk over to a full-length mirror. You begin to hear the words that you usually speak to yourself. You know the words - the ones that are so mean to you and words that *don't* validate your immense awesomeness.

Before you can get a complete sentence out, you say, "Stop!"

You look at yourself in the mirror. You look into your eyes. You say, "I love you." Maybe it is an emotional statement for you to make to yourself, and that is okay. Then, you look deeper into your eyes, and you say, "I love you" again.

(pause 5 seconds)

Keep looking into your eyes and meaningfully saying, "I love you." Allow yourself to really feel this love and to be okay with receiving this love. You deserve love from you more than anyone else.

(pause 20 seconds)

Now imagine yourself transforming in the mirror. You are going from where you started to the authentic version of yourself.

(pause 10 seconds)

Maybe your shoulders push back, your spine straightens, a knowing smile crosses your face, and your eyes... oh, your eyes. They begin to sparkle.

(pause 10 seconds)

What kind of clothes are you wearing now? What kind of friends surround you? What are you doing with your time? How do you appear to the outside world?

Take a few moments and allow this beautiful transformation to unfold before your eyes.

(pause 60 seconds)

You take a deep breath, turn around, and fling open the door from the room you were in.

You step outside into the world and shine. You shine so brightly! Like-minded people are drawn to you and you to them. You are showing your true colors, and it feels so good. It creates so much happiness in your heart. You, free to be you, can live the life you came here to live!

Now, open those beautiful butterfly wings and fly wherever you want to go. This is what you wanted for yourself when you came to earth. You are free to be you.

**

(quicken your voice and allow it to sound more upbeat and normal)

You've done a very good job today! You have successfully established what your life is. A life filled with love, happiness, and all the wonderful things love and happiness holds for you.

It's time to start to wiggle your toes... your fingers... start to move your body a little bit...

When you are ready, you can open your eyes.

Living Peace & Joy Visualization

Welcome to your visualization. You deserve this time to create the life you want for yourself.

As you settle into a position that is comfortable for you, start to notice your breath.

(pause 15 seconds)

There is no need to control it or make it slower. In fact, you may notice that simply by *noticing* your breath, it will begin to slow, and perhaps it will deepen as well.

(pause 5 seconds)

Just keep noticing your breath...

(pause 5 seconds)

When a thought comes to your mind, notice that it is there, release it, and go back to your breath.

(pause 20 seconds)

Now, as you breathe in, imagine a beautiful glow of the color you choose, being inhaled and filling your entire body.

(pause 10 seconds)

As you exhale, release any negativity you may have built up inside of you. Your exhales are a great time to make sure your body is all relaxed, and you release any tensions in your muscles.

(pause 10 seconds)

Remember, with each inhale, you are growing the beautiful glow... it fills your body so much it starts to surround your body and maybe even fill the room you're in right now.

(pause 20 seconds)

This glow is the glow of pure love. You have pure love filling your body and surrounding your body.

Keep breathing. Keep noticing the beautiful, growing glow. Keep releasing any negativity and tensions.

The next time you hear my voice, we will begin the visualization process to create the life you want...

(pause 30 seconds)

**

Briefly imagine a situation that brings you frustration of some sort. Don't let yourself get *into the emotion*; just pick a situation. Maybe it's while you're driving, speaking with a particular person, trying to accomplish a task you're not the best at, or something else.

(pause 10 seconds)

Now, imagine what it would look like if you could get through that situation with a sense of peace and joy. As if whatever used to trigger you no longer has a hold on you.

Imagine the event happening, and you staying calm and happy with a smile on your face.

(pause 10 seconds)

Really think about it and imagine it happening. If you'd like, you can even imagine little cartoon hearts surrounding you and you breathing out a glittery plume of air... anything that takes this situation over the top in terms of how well you react... take a few moments and allow that scenario to build in your mind.

(pause 20 seconds)

Peace and joy are always with you. But, if you aren't currently living in peace and joy, they are only a thought away.

Imagine how satisfying your life will be when you can choose peace and joy at any moment.

(pause 10 seconds)

It is as if you are floating right above the earth, with gladness in your eyes and peace in your heart.

You can float right past an unpleasant situation and spread your peaceful and joyful ambiance as you go by, leaving others with that incredible sensation of peace and joy as well.

Let's build an image in your mind of going through your day with you living peacefully and joyfully.

You wake up, and a smile crosses your face. You know you will easily navigate your way through your day.

Now, continue with how your day usually proceeds and imagine approaching your life with peace and joy. Make sure to include how you view *yourself* and your interaction with others.

(pause 40 seconds)

Isn't it nice to know that you are in complete control of your life? You can live in peace and joy simply by choosing it.

It's okay if, at first, you choose it on a moment-by-moment basis. Soon, you will be at the point where you simply live your life in peace and joy; but for now, you simply choose it.

If something happens that triggers your old thinking - other than peace and joy - imagine your cartoon hearts and glittery breath taking over the situation...

(pause 10 seconds)

Not only will *you* be living in peace and joy, but you will spread it all around you, allowing others to feel it too. So take a moment to imagine how wonderful that is to have everyone around you living in peace and joy as well...

(pause 20 seconds)

Throughout your day, remember peace and joy and hearts and glitter breath. They surround you and follow you wherever you go. You simply need to think about them and choose to let them lead your way.

**

(quicken your voice and allow it to sound more upbeat and normal)

You've done a very good job today! You have successfully established what your life is. A life filled with love, happiness, and all the wonderful things love and happiness holds for you.

It's time to start to wiggle your toes... your fingers... start to move your body a little bit...

When you are ready, you can open your eyes.

Life's Balance
Visualization

Welcome to your visualization. You deserve this time to create the life you want for yourself.

As you settle into a position that is comfortable for you, start to notice your breath.

(pause 15 seconds)

There is no need to control it or make it slower. In fact, you may notice that simply by *noticing* your breath, it will begin to slow, and perhaps it will deepen as well.

(pause 5 seconds)

Just keep noticing your breath...

(pause 5 seconds)

When a thought comes to your mind, notice that it is there, release it, and go back to your breath.

(pause 20 seconds)

Now, as you breathe in, imagine a beautiful glow of the color you choose, being inhaled and filling your entire body.

(pause 10 seconds)

As you exhale, release any negativity you may have built up inside of you. Your exhales are a great time to make sure your body is all relaxed, and you release any tensions in your muscles.

(pause 10 seconds)

Remember, with each inhale, you are growing the beautiful glow... it fills your body so much it starts to surround your body and maybe even fill the room you're in right now.

(pause 20 seconds)

This glow is the glow of pure love. You have pure love filling your body and surrounding your body.

Keep breathing. Keep noticing the beautiful, growing glow. Keep releasing any negativity and tensions.

The next time you hear my voice, we will begin the visualization process to create the life you want...

(pause 30 seconds)

**

Take a moment here to think about two things that are most important to you in your life. Make sure it is what *you* find importance in, not what you *think* you should find important. It could be your health, happiness, finances, family, or anything else. Think about what two things are most important to you...

(pause 15 seconds)

Think about what two things you find fun. Of course, this varies greatly for each person, so pick the two things that *you* find fun.

(pause 15 seconds)

Now, think about the things you absolutely must do in the course of a week. Again, these are things that *you* feel are without a doubt very important you get done. Maybe it's work, chores, laundry, cooking at home, social interaction... it's entirely up to you. Pick your top two things that you absolutely must get done in the week.

(pause 15 seconds)

To live a balanced life, you want to make sure to incorporate all of those things without feeling overwhelmed or burning yourself out. This is totally doable.

Recall the two things that are most important to you... the two things that you find fun... and the two things you must get done in a week.

(pause 10 seconds)

Take a moment to think about those six different things with neutral eyes - they are what they are, nothing more, nothing less...

(pause 10 seconds)

If you were to look at your week as a whole, how can you see yourself accomplishing all of those things? Take a moment to think about that and what your balanced week looks like. Make sure to see how happy you are having all of those things accomplished.

(pause 30 seconds)

These six things are imperative to your balanced life... getting them done, even though one or more may be something you don't enjoy doing at the moment... will lead to you feeling balanced and accomplished.

See yourself having done all six of these things at the end of your week. How does that feel to you? Take a moment to feel how nice it is to have your life in balance.

(pause 20 seconds)

It is very important that you schedule these six things into your week. If you are asked to do something else, and it will mean you can't accomplish any one of these six priorities in your life, tell the person, "no."

Imagine somebody asking you to do something that won't fit into your week. How might you tell that person no? Then, imagine Imagine yourself telling them no with love in your heart.

(pause 10 seconds)

You are important. Your desires are important. Your time is important. You feeling balanced in your life is important.

Imagine yourself on top of a hill, with valleys all around you. As you stand there, a slight breeze blows your hair behind you. The sunshine comfortably warms your face. You raise your hands in a humble victory, proud of yourself for accomplishing balance in your life.

(pause 15 seconds)

**

(quicken your voice and allow it to sound more upbeat and normal)

You've done a very good job today! You have successfully established what your life is. A life filled with love, happiness, and all the wonderful things love and happiness holds for you.

It's time to start to wiggle your toes... your fingers... start to move your body a little bit...

When you are ready, you can open your eyes.

My Highest & Best Potential for Fulfillment Visualization

Welcome to your visualization. You deserve this time to create the life you want for yourself.

As you settle into a position that is comfortable for you, start to notice your breath.

(pause 15 seconds)

There is no need to control it or make it slower. In fact, you may notice that simply by *noticing* your breath, it will begin to slow, and perhaps it will deepen as well.

(pause 5 seconds)

Just keep noticing your breath...

(pause 5 seconds)

When a thought comes to your mind, notice that it is there, release it, and go back to your breath.

(pause 20 seconds)

Now, as you breathe in, imagine a beautiful glow of the color you choose, being inhaled and filling your entire body.

(pause 10 seconds)

As you exhale, release any negativity you may have built up inside of you. Your exhales are a great time to make sure your body is all relaxed, and you release any tensions in your muscles.

(pause 10 seconds)

Remember, with each inhale, you are growing the beautiful glow... it fills your body so much it starts to surround your body and maybe even fill the room you're in right now.

(pause 20 seconds)

This glow is the glow of pure love. You have pure love filling your body and surrounding your body.

Keep breathing. Keep noticing the beautiful, growing glow. Keep releasing any negativity and tensions.

The next time you hear my voice, we will begin the visualization process to create the life you want...

(pause 30 seconds)

**

Imagine you are someplace you find very relaxing. Notice everything around you, and feel how relaxed your body and mind are while you're there.

(pause 15 seconds)

It is time to leave behind old stories that you've told yourself about what is or isn't possible for you and your life. You have all the potential with you. Anything is possible, and it all starts with creating *new* stories for you to live your life by.

You begin thinking about what you're doing when you're having the most fun. See and feel yourself doing it, and take a moment to think about what that activity *is* that is so much fun for you.

(pause 15 seconds)

Now, think about what *makes* that fun for you. It could be because it is exciting to you; it could bring about happiness or bliss. Maybe it is fun for you because it makes you think or because you provide help for somebody else. There are so many reasons why that activity could be fun for you. Take a moment to pinpoint at least one reason why.

(pause 20 seconds)

Take that reason why your fun activity is so much fun for you, and think about ways you can work that reason into your daily life. So, if your fun activity makes you feel blissful, what can you do right now, without changing much of your life, that will bring about the feeling of bliss? Take a moment to see how you can work that feeling into your daily life.

(pause 20 seconds)

Now begin to let your thoughts wander into what *bigger* thing you could do to bring about that feeling. It could be creating a business, starting a movement, joining a club, being creative... whatever you can imagine that would allow this feeling, this *result* of your fun activity, to be a very large part of your life. Allow your thoughts to touch on anything that comes about and see where it takes you, and allow this to happen without judgment...

(pause 30 seconds)

You now have established what you do for fun, the feeling that *makes* it fun, how you can fit that feeling into your daily life, and possible ways you take that fun reason into a large part of your life...

Think how all of those make you feel. Really feel that feeling now.

(pause 15 seconds)

Now, imagine yourself back in your very relaxing place. You notice a *being* before you. There is no fear, only love. This is your higher self coming to speak to you about all of the wonderful things you just established.

What does your higher self say to you about living your life according to this *feeling*? Allow the next several minutes to be filled with a conversation between *you* and your higher self.

(pause 120 seconds)

Your highest and best potential for fulfillment is always available to you. It is up to you to allow it to become a part of your life, and you can easily do that.

**

(quicken your voice and allow it to sound more upbeat and normal)

You've done a very good job today! You have successfully established what your life is. A life filled with love, happiness, and all the wonderful things love and happiness holds for you.

It's time to start to wiggle your toes... your fingers... start to move your body a little bit...

When you are ready, you can open your eyes.

The Confidence Critter Visualization

Welcome to your visualization. You deserve this time to create the life you want for yourself.

As you settle into a position that is comfortable for you, start to notice your breath.

(pause 15 seconds)

There is no need to control it or make it slower. In fact, you may notice that simply by *noticing* your breath, it will begin to slow, and perhaps it will deepen as well.

(pause 5 seconds)

Just keep noticing your breath...

(pause 5 seconds)

When a thought comes to your mind, notice that it is there, release it, and go back to your breath.

(pause 20 seconds)

Now, as you breathe in, imagine a beautiful glow of the color you choose, being inhaled and filling your entire body.

(pause 10 seconds)

As you exhale, release any negativity you may have built up inside of you. Your exhales are a great time to make sure your body is all relaxed, and you release any tensions in your muscles.

(pause 10 seconds)

Remember, with each inhale, you are growing the beautiful glow... it fills your body so much it starts to surround your body and maybe even fill the room you're in right now.

(pause 20 seconds)

This glow is the glow of pure love. You have pure love filling your body and surrounding your body.

Keep breathing. Keep noticing the beautiful, growing glow. Keep releasing any negativity and tensions.

The next time you hear my voice, we will begin the visualization process to create the life you want...

(pause 30 seconds)

**

Conjure up an image of an animal that you adore. It can be a specific pet or an animal like a cat, a bird, or even a giraffe. This little critter exudes nothing but love for you. Imagine it to be big enough to fit on your shoulder and stay there all day in the image you're creating. It can be a cartoon image or look like the actual critter.

(pause 20seconds)

There is a secret to this critter; it is *magical*! It always knows the perfect time to give you an extra burst of confidence! That's why we'll call it your Confidence Critter! This confidence it gives to you comes from a grand source of love, acceptance, and happiness. All you need to do to get this burst of confidence is to think about your Confidence Critter, and it will all be yours.

Bring to mind an instance when you aren't feeling very confident. It's okay to feel doubt, fear, or hesitation a little bit, but don't let it overtake you. Think about this situation for just a moment.

(pause 15 seconds)

Now, take a quick glance at your Confidence Critter, sitting on your shoulder. That little animal is just *beaming* at you!

It *knows* you can handle this situation with confidence, grace, and love, and it exudes its special magic into your vibration, and you take on an entirely different personality! You are confident!

Go back to the instance where you weren't feeling very confident, and now relive the same situation with the magic of your Confidence Critter!

(pause 20 seconds)

You shine! You sparkle! You rock! You walk away from whatever your situation is with such a stride of confidence, and you *know* you *nailed* it!

We're going to go through several different scenarios. With each one, imagine you with your Confidence Critter on your shoulder and see just how confident you handle the situation...

You are speaking in front of an audience. *(pause 15 seconds)*

You are going to the doctor. *(pause 15 seconds)*

You are talking about your finances. *(pause 15 seconds)*

You are naked. *(pause 15 seconds)*

You are facing a fear. *(pause 15 seconds)*

You look in the mirror. *(pause 15 seconds)*

No matter what you do in life, your Confidence Critter will be right there for you, on your shoulder, waiting for you to think about it so it can release that magical confidence to you.

**

(quicken your voice and allow it to sound more upbeat and normal)

You've done a very good job today! You have successfully established what your life is. A life filled with love, happiness, and all the wonderful things love and happiness holds for you.

It's time to start to wiggle your toes... your fingers... start to move your body a little bit... When you are ready, you can open your eyes.

Have Fun!
Visualization

Welcome to your visualization. You deserve this time to create the life you want for yourself.

As you settle into a position that is comfortable for you, start to notice your breath.

(pause 15 seconds)

There is no need to control it or make it slower. In fact, you may notice that simply by *noticing* your breath, it will begin to slow, and perhaps it will deepen as well.

(pause 5 seconds)

Just keep noticing your breath...

(pause 5 seconds)

When a thought comes to your mind, notice that it is there, release it, and go back to your breath.

(pause 20 seconds)

Now, as you breathe in, imagine a beautiful glow of the color you choose, being inhaled and filling your entire body.

(pause 10 seconds)

As you exhale, release any negativity you may have built up inside of you. Your exhales are a great time to make sure your body is all relaxed, and you release any tensions in your muscles.

(pause 10 seconds)

141

Remember, with each inhale, you are growing the beautiful glow... it fills your body so much it starts to surround your body and maybe even fill the room you're in right now.

(pause 20 seconds)

This glow is the glow of pure love. You have pure love filling your body and surrounding your body.

Keep breathing. Keep noticing the beautiful, growing glow. Keep releasing any negativity and tensions.

The next time you hear my voice, we will begin the visualization process to create the life you want...

(pause 30 seconds)

**

Today is going to be such a fun day for you! You get to choose exactly what you're going to do, if you're going to have anyone with you, what you're going to wear and more.

Allow yourself to choose *anything* you want to do, and remember what may be fun for others doesn't necessarily mean it is fun for you, so maybe fun for you today is sitting in a coffee shop with your laptop, or perhaps you'll choose to go ziplining. Anything goes here. It is all for you, and it is all in your hands.

Start by deciding what fun thing you want to do today.

(pause 15 seconds)

Before you begin your fun, you've got to pick out what you will wear. Is it pajamas... jeans... or maybe you're dressing up for an elegant time? Imagine your outfit now...

(pause 15 seconds)

If you are leaving your house, are you going to make any additional stops, or are you going straight to your place of fun? Imagine all of that now...

(pause 20 seconds)

Are you enjoying this fun alone or with others?

(pause 15 seconds)

Now that you have all of the parameters decided, it's time to begin your fun time.

The rest of this visualization is for you to create the picture of you getting ready, making sure you have everything you need, and pursuing your fun! Take time to really get into it and allow yourself to see what is happening, to feel what is happening, to smell and taste and hear all that is around you... Feeling your emotions with this fun time is a major bonus, so allow the smiles, the laughter, and the happy tears.

A chime will sound after four minutes. If you'd like to continue, please do. There will be no other words spoken.

(wait four minutes)

(chime)

Today I Am Mindful Visualization

Welcome to your visualization. You deserve this time to create the life you want for yourself.

As you settle into a position that is comfortable for you, start to notice your breath.

(pause 15 seconds)

There is no need to control it or make it slower. In fact, you may notice that simply by *noticing* your breath, it will begin to slow, and perhaps it will deepen as well.

(pause 5 seconds)

Just keep noticing your breath...

(pause 5 seconds)

When a thought comes to your mind, notice that it is there, release it, and go back to your breath.

(pause 20 seconds)

Now, as you breathe in, imagine a beautiful glow of the color you choose, being inhaled and filling your entire body.

(pause 10 seconds)

As you exhale, release any negativity you may have built up inside of you. Your exhales are a great time to make sure your body is all relaxed, and you release any tensions in your muscles.

(pause 10 seconds)

Remember, with each inhale, you are growing the beautiful glow... it fills your body so much it starts to surround your body and maybe even fill the room you're in right now.

(pause 20 seconds)

This glow is the glow of pure love. You have pure love filling your body and surrounding your body.

Keep breathing. Keep noticing the beautiful, growing glow. Keep releasing any negativity and tensions.

The next time you hear my voice, we will begin the visualization process to create the life you want...

(pause 30 seconds)

**

We are about to go through four different ways you can create mindfulness. They are through breath, through concentration, through being aware of your body, and through releasing tension in your body.

Before we begin, know that it is perfectly natural for your mindfulness activity to be interrupted by your thoughts. The key is when you notice you are thinking about something, simply redirect your attention to the mindful activity.

We will start with being mindful through your breath. You don't *need* to change your breathing, but it helps to keep you more mindful if you do. The important thing is to notice how the air feels when you inhale, how it feels right *before* you exhale, how it feels *when* you exhale and how it feels when you pause before your next breath. For the next couple of minutes, focus on your breath. If you'd like, you can follow this breathing routine...

Inhale for a slow count of four...

(pause 4 seconds)

Hold for a slow count of four...

(pause 4 seconds)

Exhale for a slow count of four...

(pause 4 seconds)

Pause for a slow count of four...

Continue focusing on your breath until you hear my voice again.

(pause 1 minute 45 seconds)

Now we are going to *concentrate* on something to be mindful. Imagine a candle's flame flickering. It may dance because of airflow around it, or it may simply flicker. You will focus on this image of a candle flame for a few minutes. Remember, when your thinking brain starts to think, just go back to your candle flame when you notice your thought. Continue to do this until you hear my voice again.

(pause 2 minutes)

Now it's time to create mindfulness through *being aware of your body.* This is easiest done when you feel your body move with your breath. With each inhale and exhale, feel how your body moves. See how far down your body you can feel your breath. Then, again, when your thoughts wander, just bring your attention back to your breath, moving your body. Do this for about two minutes until you hear my voice again.

(pause 2 minutes)

Take a deep cleansing breath in, and when you release it, allow your muscles to melt and release. Doing this is being mindful through *releasing tension in your body.*

If you feel anywhere that is especially tight, take a moment and really feel those muscles relax...

Now, we will start releasing individual sets of muscles.

Release your face muscles.

(pause 5 seconds)

Release your neck muscles.

(pause 5 seconds)

Your shoulders.

(pause 5 seconds)

Your arms and hands...

(pause 5 seconds)
Your chest... Your torso
(pause 5 seconds)
Release your abdomen muscles and your backside muscles.
(pause 5 seconds)
Now release your thighs... your knees... your calves.
(pause 5 seconds)
Release your feet and your toe muscles...
(pause 5 seconds)
You've done a very good job today being mindful.
**

(quicken your voice and allow it to sound more upbeat and normal)

You've done a very good job today! You have successfully established what your life is. A life filled with love, happiness, and all the wonderful things love and happiness holds for you.

It's time to start to wiggle your toes... your fingers... start to move your body a little bit...

When you are ready, you can open your eyes.

Give Love. Receive Love. Visualization

Welcome to your visualization. You deserve this time to create the life you want for yourself.

As you settle into a position that is comfortable for you, start to notice your breath.

(pause 15 seconds)

There is no need to control it or make it slower. In fact, you may notice that simply by *noticing* your breath, it will begin to slow, and perhaps it will deepen as well.

(pause 5 seconds)

Just keep noticing your breath...

(pause 5 seconds)

When a thought comes to your mind, notice that it is there, release it, and go back to your breath.

(pause 20 seconds)

Now, as you breathe in, imagine a beautiful glow of the color you choose, being inhaled and filling your entire body.

(pause 10 seconds)

As you exhale, release any negativity you may have built up inside of you. Your exhales are a great time to make sure your body is all relaxed, and you release any tensions in your muscles.

(pause 10 seconds)

Remember, with each inhale, you are growing the beautiful glow... it fills your body so much it starts to surround your body and maybe even fill the room you're in right now.

(pause 20 seconds)

This glow is the glow of pure love. You have pure love filling your body and surrounding your body.

Keep breathing. Keep noticing the beautiful, growing glow. Keep releasing any negativity and tensions.

The next time you hear my voice, we will begin the visualization process to create the life you want...

(pause 30 seconds)

**

Bring to mind a person you know. It doesn't matter who. If you want to focus more on forgiveness, bring to mind somebody you are upset with. If you want to focus on growing pure love, bring to mind somebody you love. Maybe you even bring to mind a stranger that you know could use some extra love and support. Now bring to mind that person...

(pause 10 seconds)

With their face in mind, strip away their stories. Strip away their personality. Just see them for who they truly are. See them as a human being, living life on earth as well as they know how. If you can, change their image to them as a child. Take a few moments to allow this to happen in your mind's image.

(pause 20 seconds)

Now that you see them as a pure human spirit, realize all they want, deep down, is love. Pure love. Look into their eyes and see the purity of their spirit.

(pause 10 seconds)

As you look into their eyes, allow yourself to feel your connection with them. We are all one, and while you *are* looking at them, you also can recognize yourself in their eyes as well.

Now start showering them with love. Imagine hearts being bombarded at them. You can even make it fun if you'd like and see them playfully catching the hearts and pulling them into their bodies.

(pause 15 seconds)

Next, send them vibrations of love, penetrating their skin like the sun on a hot day.

(pause 15 seconds)

Imagine a loving, glittery red glow encapsulating them. You can see them filled with love - a love so deep and so pure that they are not only blissful but taken to a level they have forgotten since being born.

(pause 15 seconds)

You are sending them the love of unity — the love of peace, joy, and enlightenment.

You see them beam with this love! They are truly living their most authentic spirit with all of this love!

Now that you have filled them with such an indescribable sensation, they are beyond capable of sending that same love back to you.

Imagine them sending you hearts and you pulling those hearts into your body.

(pause 15 seconds)

Imagine them sending you penetrating vibrations of love.

(pause 15 seconds)

Imagine that red glittery glow encapsulating *you* as well.

(pause 15 seconds)

Anytime you need some of this love, all you need to do is first send it to somebody else and then allow them to send it back to you.

You are so worthy of love; after all, it's what you *are*.

**

(quicken your voice and allow it to sound more upbeat and normal)

You've done a very good job today! You have successfully established what your life is. A life filled with love, happiness, and all the wonderful things love and happiness holds for you.

It's time to start to wiggle your toes... your fingers... start to move your body a little bit...

When you are ready, you can open your eyes.

I Am Health Visualization

Welcome to your visualization. You deserve this time to create the life you want for yourself.

As you settle into a position that is comfortable for you, start to notice your breath.

(pause 15 seconds)

There is no need to control it or make it slower. In fact, you may notice that simply by *noticing* your breath, it will begin to slow, and perhaps it will deepen as well.

(pause 5 seconds)

Just keep noticing your breath...

(pause 5 seconds)

When a thought comes to your mind, notice that it is there, release it, and go back to your breath.

(pause 20 seconds)

Now, as you breathe in, imagine a beautiful glow of the color you choose, being inhaled and filling your entire body.

(pause 10 seconds)

As you exhale, release any negativity you may have built up inside of you. Your exhales are a great time to make sure your body is all relaxed, and you release any tensions in your muscles.

(pause 10 seconds)

Remember, with each inhale, you are growing the beautiful glow... it fills your body so much it starts to surround your body and maybe even fill the room you're in right now.

(pause 20 seconds)

This glow is the glow of pure love. You have pure love filling your body and surrounding your body.

Keep breathing. Keep noticing the beautiful, growing glow. Keep releasing any negativity and tensions.

The next time you hear my voice, we will begin the visualization process to create the life you want...

(pause 30 seconds)

**

Imagine yourself walking through a beautiful garden — a garden where you feel so safe and so peaceful.

(pause 10 seconds)

The weather is absolutely perfect for you. It's the kind of day you *live* for.

You see all kinds of trees with birds flying from branch to branch as you look around. The songs the birds sing lull you into a space of simple happiness.

(pause 5 seconds)

And the flowers! There are so many flowers. It seems like the more you look around, the more flowers you see!

(pause 5 seconds)

Suddenly, a little fairy appears before you. You are surprised and intrigued by her arrival. She calls you closer to her, and when you get as close as you can, she takes her magic wand and touches the top of your head. A sensation runs down your body, from your head, all the way to your toes, and you realize you can fly! In fact, your feet are already off of the ground.

She starts flying, and you follow her. You have so much fun, you and the fairy, flying around this gorgeous garden, making loops in the air, and smelling flower scents as you fly by them. What an absolute joyful time.

(pause 20 seconds)

The fairy takes you to her home. It's a tiny hole in a tree. She flies through the door and laughs as you try to fly into her home, but only your nose fits. Finally, she pushes your nose out of her door and sits next to you, at the base of possibly the most giant tree you have ever seen.

She then begins to tell you that you are in the magic garden of health. Anything and everything you could ever want for the health of your physical and emotional well-being is yours for the taking in this garden, but you *are not* to focus on that fact. Instead, you are instructed to fly around and smell *alllll* the flowers. When you find an aroma you like, take that flower and put it in your pocket. The fairy explains that picking the flower is okay because another one immediately replaces it.

Take a moment to fly around this magical garden while picking the flowers with the most amazing scents... Also, make sure you notice the butterflies, the waterfall, and the shimmering creek while you are on your adventure!

(pause 60 seconds)

You've picked a *lot* of flowers, so you decide to head back to the fairy's home. When you get there, she clues you in on some big magic. She tells you that you intuitively *know* what flowers to pick that will heal your health woes. You picked exactly what you needed to become the healthiest version of yourself that you could imagine! In fact, the healing has already started to take place. Just by focusing on the good things in life, health seems to appear automatically.

She goes on to tell you that you simply need to smell the flowers, notice the beauty all around you, and know in your heart that your healing is intuitive, magical, automatic.

**

(quicken your voice and allow it to sound more upbeat and normal)

You've done a very good job today! You have successfully established what your life is. A life filled with love, happiness, and all the wonderful things love and happiness holds for you.

It's time to start to wiggle your toes... your fingers... start to move your body a little bit...

When you are ready, you can open your eyes.

NOTES, THOUGHTS & IDEAS

_____
_____
_____
_____
_____
_____
_____
_____
_____
_____
_____
_____
_____
_____
_____
_____
_____
_____
_____
_____
_____
_____

Affirmations

Holy cow, you have a lot of affirmations to choose from! Pick one a day, one a week, one a month, one an hour... whatever feels good to you! After picking your affirmation, put it on your mirror, the fridge, your computer monitor, as your phone wallpaper, in your car, or wherever you will see it regularly. The key to affirmations is to get *so* comfortable with them that they become second nature to you. You'll see or hear them and think, "Of course!" So say them, write them, or record them and listen to them repeatedly. Whatever you have to do to get them into the creases of your mind.

It is important to do this because we all have negative thoughts, beliefs, and programming in different areas of our lives. It's time to boot out the bad and install the new! Remember, your reality is what you make it, so these affirmations are essential!

If you'd like to create your own affirmations, remember to state them in the present tense.

State it like this: "I AM a wealthy, healthy, happy person!"

NOT based in the future like this: "I WILL BE a wealthy, healthy, happy person!"

If you have trouble believing an "I am" statement, take the ownership out of it and just state the fact. Instead of: "I am strong and healthy." Make it: "Strong and Healthy."

List of Affirmations

Abundance is all around me.

Each day in every way, I get better and better.

Growing older is a gift, and I do so with grace and love.

I accept 100% responsibility for my life.

I accept myself.

I accept others.

I allow abundance into my life.

I allow goodness into my life.

I allow happiness into my life.

I allow health into my life.

I allow love into my life.

I allow my most profound questions to receive answers.

I allow my dreams to unfold for me.

I allow the flow of money into my life.

I am 100% my authentic self.

I am abundant.

I am amazingly unique, and I love that.

I am beautiful and amazing.

I am beautiful inside and out.

I am brave.

I am calm, content, and happy.

I am capable.

I am confident.

I am constantly growing.

I am creative.

I am enough.
I am everything I need for my success.
I am excited about the future.
I am focused.
I am freaking fantastic.
I am free to be me.
I am funny.
I am grateful.
I am growing at my perfect pace.
I am happy.
I am healing every second.
I am healthy.
I am here to create, play and love.
I am in control of my life.
I am in the perfect space for me right now.
I am intelligent.
I am love.
I am making today count.
I am mindful.
I am motivated.
I am open to new ideas.
I am open.
I am optimistic.
I am peaceful.
I am powerful.
I am self-aware.
I am strong.
I am succeeding more and more.
I am successful.
I am unique and important.
I am unstoppable.
I am valued and helpful.
I am weird and wonderful.
I am worth self-care.

I am worthy of abundance.

I am worthy of adoration.

I am worthy of respect.

I appreciate my body.

I appreciate the little things in life.

I ask for help.

I attract abundance into my life.

I attract health into my life.

I attract joy into my life.

I attract love into my life.

I attract peace into my life.

I believe in myself.

I can achieve absolutely anything.

I can achieve anything.

I can become anything I decide to become.

I can quickly quiet my thoughts through breath.

I celebrate the differences in others.

I choose happiness.

I choose health.

I choose love.

I choose my life with the stories I tell myself.

I choose peace.

I choose to be happy.

I choose wealth.

I contribute value to the world.

I control how I react.

I deserve to take up space.

I do my best, and that is enough.

I do something - even if I don't know what to do.

I do what feels good deep down.

I easily connect to concepts larger than myself.

I easily find things I'm grateful for.

I easily forgive myself.

I easily forgive others.

I easily live a balanced life.

I embrace my day.

I embrace my true self.

I encourage myself.

I encourage others.

I enjoy new experiences.

I exude happiness and love.

I feel good.

I feel peaceful and whole.

I find energy in my natural environment.

I find happiness in anything.

I find it easy to set boundaries when needed.

I focus on the positive.

I focus on what I desire.

I fully live each day.

I handle anything that comes my way.

I have a healthy body, and it gets healthier and healthier.

I have endless opportunities.

I have everything I need to succeed.

I have the power to create change.

I have unlimited potential.

I inhale happiness and exhale doubt.

I inhale health and exhale physical and emotional pain.

I inhale love and exhale negativity.

I inspire other people.

I listen to the universe.

I love my body.

I love my life from a place of love.

I love myself for exactly who I am.

I make a significant difference in the lives of others.

I make choices that make me proud.

I nourish my body.

I release what I no longer need or want.

I respect myself.

I respect others.
I seek people who feel safe to me.
I speak kindly to myself.
I speak kindly to others.
I speak my needs.
I step out of my comfort zone with vigor.
I take time to enjoy the seasons.
I treat myself with respect.
I view problems as opportunities.
I watch my thoughts.
It is easy for me to let go of what no longer serves me.
It is okay to change my mind.
My feelings and emotions are valid.
My life gets better as I get older.
My needs and wants are important.
My past does not define my future.
Others love to be around me.
Today I can start anything.
Today I will do my best.
Today is a great day.
Today is freaking awesome.
Today is fun.
Today is productive.
Today is the day I create the life I want.

NOTES, THOUGHTS & IDEAS

_____
_____
_____
_____
_____
_____
_____
_____
_____
_____
_____
_____
_____
_____
_____
_____
_____
_____

NOTES, THOUGHTS & IDEAS

_____
_____
_____
_____
_____
_____
_____
_____
_____
_____
_____
_____
_____
_____
_____
_____
_____
_____
_____

Section 3 - Go-To Practices

There are a lot of standard practices that are very effective, yet we tend to let them slide with the hustle of life. The more of these you can make a part of your daily (or weekly) practice, the happier you will be. Plus, you will gain the confidence that you are, indeed, a powerful being!

Ho'oponopono

Ho'oponopono is the ancient Hawaiian prayer of forgiveness. It is based on the law that we create our own reality, so anything "bad" that has happened to us, we have allowed it to happen. This short prayer allows you to take responsibility for your actions and offer yourself forgiveness.

Brain Dump Pages

Brain dump pages are when you set a timer or set an allotted amount of pages to write, and you simply write every thought in your head. This is very effective in helping you feel better, and the more you do it, you will even easily get solutions to your problems!

Journaling & Journaling Prompts

Journaling is a cathartic activity that allows you to create, record, and relish the day. The more you journal, the more you will get to know yourself, and knowing yourself is crucial to being happy. You will also find prompts that will jump-start your journaling!

Future Journaling & Future Journaling Prompts

Future journaling is writing as if you are already the person you want to become. For example, do you want to climb Mt. Everest? You would write about the lessons you learned, the most beautiful scenery you saw, and the friends you made on your journey. Included are prompts to get your future journaling off to a great start!

Visualization and Visualization Menu

Visualizing is a valuable tool in becoming all you could ever dream of! Much like Future Journaling, you visualize yourself as already having achieved what you want in your life.

Planning

Planning is an old-school tool, but it can help you get your footing and take off running! We all believe we can't snap our fingers and achieve our goals. But, planning your route to achievement will give you the steps you want to take toward the future you want.

Feel Your Way

While this is a very simple practice, it will undoubtedly change your life for the better! It's all about feeling your way to the happy life you desire.

Self Expression

What is life for if not to express your individuality? We are here to be happy and to soar! Being true to yourself is vital, and when you do this, you will free your spirit in a way that is impossible with any other practice.

Gratitude

Gratitude will increase your happiness in ways beyond measure! The more you do it, the more you will see the rewards, and you will begin to open up to life in a way you've never done before.

NOTES, THOUGHTS & IDEAS

_____
_____
_____
_____
_____
_____
_____
_____
_____
_____
_____
_____
_____
_____
_____
_____
_____
_____
_____
_____
_____

NOTES, THOUGHTS & IDEAS

_____
_____
_____
_____
_____
_____
_____
_____
_____
_____
_____
_____
_____
_____
_____
_____
_____
_____
_____
_____
_____
_____
_____
_____
_____

Ho'oponopono

Ho'oponopono is the ancient Hawaiian prayer of forgiveness. It is based on the law that we create our own reality, so anything "bad" that has happened to us, we have allowed it to happen. This short prayer allows you to take responsibility for your actions and offer yourself forgiveness.

It may seem rather odd to think you are responsible for the things in your life that haven't gone the way you'd like them to go. Why would you want to be afflicted with a health ailment, a strained relationship, lack of finances, etc.? It's not so much that you want the issue in your life, but instead, you desire (on a deep, unseen & unknown level) some kind of knowledge of how you will deal with that issue. Perhaps you will learn how to connect to yourself on a level you've always desired, learn how to speak your truth, or countless other positive possibilities.

Another way to look at taking responsibility for everything that happens in your life lies in the fact that we create our own reality. We see what we expect to see. We have the experiences we expect to have. (This is why it is *so* important to know what you are thinking!) So when we take responsibility for the things that are happening or have happened, we are acknowledging the thoughts we have thought in the past, and we are ready to forgive ourselves for those thoughts and move onwards and upwards!

Reciting the Ho'oponopono prayer will help with forgiveness for yourself and others, cultivate self-love and help cleanse the feelings of guilt, shame, and negativity of all kinds. It can also help to purify and cleanse your body/mind and release bad or sad memories and emotions that can keep you stuck in life. Ultimately, the Ho'oponopono prayer can bring relief and healing to your life.

The prayer consists of four statements:

I'm sorry.
Please forgive me.
Thank you.
I love you.

If you sit quietly and repeat the prayer 7-10 times, you will be amazed at how much better you feel when you're done.

You can also bring to mind somebody who has wronged you or who you have wronged, and recite the prayer with them in mind. After doing this, you'll be amazed at how the fracture begins to heal with a kind word or deed from the other person.

It is also excellent to record the four statements and play them on repeat while you sleep. It seems to penetrate your being and become a part of you.

Another unique way to benefit from this prayer is to help heal your relationship with society, Mother Earth, and anything you want to improve your relationship with. So simply bring to mind whatever you want to heal before reciting the prayer.

NOTES, THOUGHTS & IDEAS

_____
_____
_____
_____
_____
_____
_____
_____
_____
_____
_____
_____
_____
_____
_____
_____
_____
_____
_____
_____

NOTES, THOUGHTS & IDEAS

_____
_____
_____
_____
_____
_____
_____
_____
_____
_____
_____
_____
_____
_____
_____
_____
_____
_____
_____

Brain Dump Pages

Writing Brain Dump Pages is a method to get everything rattling around in your thoughts *out* of your brain and down on paper. You set a timer or set an allotted amount of pages to write, and you simply write every thought in your head. You write all about you — your thoughts, your fears, your negativity, your anxiety, your depression, your problems, your problems with another person, your hope, your dreams, your excitement, your love, your hope... They are all about you and your thoughts about you.

Sometimes it takes a couple of times to do a brain dump before you see the benefits of doing it, but after seeing the benefit, you won't want to leave this out of your arsenal! It's like going to a therapist and not leaving one thing unsaid.

After doing a couple of brain dumps, you will begin to notice you are not only getting things out of your head, but you start dealing with things that you may have swept under the rug. And then, another strange thing happens — you start to come up with solutions to your problems or issues. The answers seemingly just come to you.

One of the most helpful hints is to keep writing. Don't stop to think of what else you will write about. If you don't know what else to write, write about the fact you don't know what else you should write about. The key is just to keep writing. Continual writing prevents you from questioning if you should put a thought on paper or not. The answer is to always put all of your thoughts on paper during a brain dump.

Chances are, you will be writing things that you never, ever want anybody else to read! Because of that, many people will write these types of pages in a throw-away notebook. Or, dump your thoughts on your paper and when you're done, re-cycle or shred them so they are gone for good and nobody will ever see them. Doing this ensures you feel safe releasing those thoughts onto paper, and getting them out of your head and onto paper is where the magic lies.

A typical amount of time to put into Brain Dump Pages is three pages worth, or about 30 minutes of writing.

NOTES, THOUGHTS & IDEAS

_____
_____
_____
_____
_____
_____
_____
_____
_____
_____
_____
_____
_____
_____
_____
_____
_____
_____
_____
_____
_____

NOTES, THOUGHTS & IDEAS

_____

_____

_____

_____

_____

_____

_____

_____

_____

_____

_____

_____

_____

_____

_____

_____

_____

_____

_____

_____

_____

_____

Journaling

Journaling is a very cathartic activity. There are several benefits to journaling like more self-esteem and confidence, helping to achieve your goals, reducing stress and anxiety, inspiring yourself, improving your mood, creativity, and mindfulness, encouraging gratitude, creating a record of your life, and so many more!

While brain dump pages get all the negativity out of your mind, journaling is all about the positive. Sure, you can journal about issues in your life, and you can even choose to be a little negative in your journal; but journaling is best when you focus on the positive.

The more you journal, the better your life gets. Journaling helps you rediscover yourself — in terms of your ego and your higher self. A consistent journaling practice will open up new doors that you wouldn't have otherwise found, and it will show you so many new possibilities in your life.

You may want to keep your journal simple, or you may want to dress it up with colored pencils, colored ink, or stickers. You may want a fancy journal, or you may choose a simple notebook. No matter what you choose, there are so many different ways you can use your journal, or you can mix and match!

Ways to use your journal:

- Planning for your future
- Nighttime dreams
- Food journaling
- Fitness journal
- To-do list
- Goals and the journey your goals take you on
- Travel journal (where you want to go or where you've been)
- The day's events
- Quotes, book excerpts, and positivity tips
- Gratitude/Things you love
- Drawing/doodling
- Plant, flower, and gardening journal
- Books you've read or notes on books you're reading
- Magic journal
- Progress you have made toward a goal journal
- Future journal (more on that in a few pages)

Journaling Tips:

- Pick a journal that feels good to you that you *know* you'll write in.
- Date each entry.
- Be honest with yourself.
- If you don't want anybody to read it - hide it.
- Allow yourself to go beyond what you think is possible in your writing.
- Make it a habit.

Journaling is *such* a treat for yourself and one you should never deny yourself.

Journaling Prompts

- What if I actually DO end up with everything I desire?
- Write about a memorable sunrise or sunset.
- What am I grateful for and why?
- What could be stopping you from reaching your goal?
- What would I do if I could do *anything* right now to bring more happiness into my life?
- What three questions do I have that I have no idea what the answers are?
- What are my top three goals, and what might I do to accomplish them?
- Write about a fun memory from when you were a kid.
- What has made you laugh so hard you cried?
- What have you done in the past couple of days that you are really proud of?
- Simply write down the happenings of yesterday or today.
- Make a grand to-do list.
- Describe your perfect day!
- What is the best gift you've ever received, and what made it special?
- Write a poem!
- You've been transported to the year 2099. What do you see, and what are things like?
- What is the number one gift *you* could give to the world?
- What if you are genuinely magical?
- How can you see a problem differently?

- Find and write down five quotes that are meaningful to you today.
- Write about what you love to do to show yourself self-care.
- Make a list of things you absolutely love.
- Describe a challenge you currently have and three different ways to work through it.
- Make a list of things you want to let go of.
- How would you most like to help somebody?
- Write an entry about what is going on in the world right now. Good and bad things!
- Create a three-month/1-year/5-year plan.
- What are the worst food and best food you've ever tried? Describe it.
- What does the *ideal* solution look like to a problem I'm currently facing?
- Write a letter to your past self, forgiving yourself for things you might have done.
- Write down three fantastic affirmations and *why* they are important to you.
- Draw your entry today - it's okay if you can't draw!
- Where will you go on your dream vacation, and what will you be sure to do while you're there?
- Write about something you are looking forward to doing.
- When do you feel you are most authentic? How can you carry that over into other parts of your life?
- Write about somebody who inspires you and why.
- What is your favorite thing about your home and why?
- What are the great qualities of somebody in your most intimate relationship?
- What if you could fly? How would it feel, and what would you do?
- If you had a magical power, what would it be, and how would you use it?

- Make a bucket list of things you want to do in the next 180 days.
- I am so grateful and happy now that...
- Make a list of great gifts to have on hand to surprise somebody with.
- In what areas are you the most creative?
- Write about changes you'd like to see in your community and how you could start that change.
- What are the most important lessons you've learned in your life?
- Write about the most persistent thing on your mind right now.
- What do you feel you *need* but do not have? Why and how might you *get* that thing?
- Write down ten things you want to do by the end of the year.
- Make a list of five different book ideas you could write.
- If you loved yourself unconditionally, how would that change what you do every day?
- What is something obscure that you would say *yes* to without hesitation.
- Write down three wishes you have.
- Make a list of random acts of kindness you'd enjoy doing.
- What is your go-to song for motivation, and why?
- If you were to look at a problematic situation in a fun way, how could you solve it?
- Write about the last book you read and what it meant to you.
- List your core values.
- If you had to evacuate your home ASAP, what three things would you grab (besides people and pets)?
- You've been sucked back to the year 1900. What is the one thing you teach people?
- Write about how you see yourself vs. how others see you.

- If your heart was doing the writing, what would it say to you today?
- Write about three things you can do to become healthier.
- What would you do if money was unlimited in your life?
- Write a letter forgiving somebody. (You don't need to send it.)
- What one trait do you wish everybody had and why?
- You can move anywhere in the world. Where is it, and why?
- What is the most important thing you have ever learned, and how have you implemented it?
- Describe how you want to be remembered and if you're living that way right now.
- Write about a recurring dream.
- What do you do to jumpstart your creativity?
- What is your most prized material possession, and why?
- What personality trait are you most proud of?
- List three challenges you currently have and three ways you can overcome them.
- Make a list of the top five people you are most grateful for and why.
- If you could go back in time, where would you go, and what would you do?
- What three books do you think everyone should read?
- If you were in charge, how would you solve homelessness?
- Write about something you thought was ridiculous until you tried it.
- What is something you *really* don't enjoy doing that most people *do* enjoy?
- What is something most people take for granted, and how can you *embrace* that thing?
- If you had *no* doubt it would work, what would you *do*?
- Describe your most ideal date night.

- Write a "day in the life of" account of *your* life if you lived somewhere entirely different.
- If you could have a conversation with *anyone*, living or dead, who would it be, and what would you talk about?
- Write about the scariest thing you've ever done and what you learned from it.
- What would you have done to be in trouble if you were on the run from the cops, and how would you hide?
- Describe the weirdest thing about you and why it's so awesome.
- Write about what your life will look like when you retire.
- What is your biggest dream, and is there a mini version of that dream you could accomplish in the next month?
- Describe what you think the afterlife is like.
- What is the next big step in your life? Are you prepared to take that step?
- Make a list of five things you are really good at.
- What is one thing you can do for yourself to create more love for yourself?
- How can you create more peace in your life?
- Write your own visualization.
- Describe what the season you're in (spring, summer, fall, winter) means to you and how you want to embrace it this year.
- What is your favorite ritual in your life right now, and what makes it so good?
- Write about an event that changed your life for the better. How different would your life be if it didn't happen?
- Who would you give money to if you had an unlimited income?
- What makes you happy?

NOTES, THOUGHTS & IDEAS

_____
_____
_____
_____
_____
_____
_____
_____
_____
_____
_____
_____
_____
_____
_____
_____
_____
_____
_____
_____
_____

Future Journaling

Future journaling is writing as if you are already the person you want to become, living the life you want to live.

Do you want to climb Mt. Everest? Then, for your future journal, you would journal about the valuable lessons you learned while training and during the climb, how you saw the most beautiful scenery you've ever seen, and all the wonderful friends you made on your journey.

The primary purpose behind future journaling is similar to visualization. If you can see it, it will come to you. When you write about your future as if it has already happened, you create an intense vision of what you want. You are recalling all the great things you have and all the wonderful things you've done.

There is one caveat, however. Almost everything you write in your future journal is a detail about what you want in your life. Things like throwing a fabulous party, donating a lot of money to a specific charity, traveling to a grand destination, and possibly taking that vacation with a specific person... All of that is very detailed when you're writing about them (as they should be).

Here's the caveat — at the end of your entry, write, "All this or something better." If you demand that your details get met, you may be selling yourself short. Plus, the details that may *actually* happen are likely to be even better than you can imagine. So, writing "All this or something better" puts your requests as a direction you'd be happy to see play out in your life.

For example, let's say you do some future journaling about the day you ran a record mile for you. You got it done in 4 minutes and 30 seconds! You crossed the finish line, and your loved ones and friends were there to meet you, and you wrapped up your day perfectly by sitting by a bonfire sipping hot tea.

If you demanded that exact scenario to play out, it may never happen because each of your loved ones may not have been able to attend.

However, if you ended it with, "All that or something better," what actually may happen is that you run a mile in 4 minutes and 20 seconds. Your loved ones and friends meet you at the finish line, but you see them after you win $5,000 for having the fastest time!

So use your future journal to excite yourself about all the things that would be so magnificent if they happened, but always allow space for something better.

You can use your future journal just like a regular journal by simply writing about your (future) day. However, if you get stuck or want to get out of your ordinary ideas, there are some Future Journal Prompts that follow.

Future Journaling Prompts

- Now that you can do whatever you want, whenever you want to do it, what are you doing?
- Now that you are comfortable with your body, these are the things on my to-do list:
- You have more than enough money for the rest of your life! Make a list of everything you'll do to your house to make it perfect for you or a buyer, or list what you must have in your *new* house. Leave out no detail!
- You are living your perfect life and making a list of all the people who helped you get where you are now and a gift you want to give them. What are you buying and who are you giving the gifts to? (If there is nobody specific, think in general terms like your realtor, agent, financial advisor, best friend, etc.)
- Yesterday and last night, you had *the* most romantic time of your life! Write about every important detail!
- Today was the first time you strolled into your doctor's office, knowing they would be amazed by how well you're doing and how healthy you are! Write about how you felt and the conversation between you and your doctor.
- Now that you are everything you've ever wanted to be, write a letter to your younger self assuring yourself that you will make it (because you did)!

- You're in line at the grocery store when somebody comes up to you with tears in their eyes. They thank you for all that you 9unknowingly) did for them. What did they say?
- Write about last week's vacation. You know, the one you always dreamed of taking! Leave nothing out!
- How did you feel when you saw your bank balance at a cool 2 million dollars?! Describe the scene.
- Today, you are receiving a fantastic award! What is it for, and what is your acceptance speech or speech notes?
- What is the special dream you had, and what steps did you take to achieve it?
- Make a to-do list you want to get done to move to your perfect, new home! Oh, and closing day is only seven days away!
- Now that you have *arrived*, what do you do to fill your days?
- You're planning a party for someone extraordinary. Who is the party for? What gift(s) will you buy for them (and maybe swag bags)? Where will the party be held? What caterers and type of food will you serve? What kind of cake will there be? Live band or DJ? Who's on the guest list?
- What three affirmations catapulted you to your perfect life? (Write them down and implement them into your life now!)
- Considering your life is pretty much exactly how you want it, describe what you see when you look in the mirror. Then, describe what you see and feel when you look deep into your eyes.
- Now that you have more money than you could dream of having, what extravagant thing do you buy for yourself?
- It is so easy for the wonderful, authentic you to shine through! What do people see when they observe you?

- You've had your perfect life for over a decade now. So what's new on the horizon for you?
- You're healthier every day. How do you celebrate and appreciate that? What foods do you cook? How do you exercise your body? Write down your favorite recipe and jot down your past week's activities.
- You're going on a trip to Bora Bora (or another place you choose)! What will you pack? What do you need to do before you leave? What are the things you must do while you're there?
- Looking back on your life, before you had everything you now have, what do you think the major turning points were for you that helped you get where you are today?
- You've realized that you didn't have to follow the rules to get where you are today. You did things differently from almost everybody else. Write about how you did it and what your journey looked like.
- If there is one thing your family and friends say changed about you since you've become the person you've always wanted to be, what would they say that thing is?
- Make a list of charities and people you've helped either financially or through volunteering - and how you helped them.
- You've just purchased 1,000 of the same widget. What is the widget? What group of people do you donate the widgets to? Why did you pick that group of people (get specific)? How does it make you feel to be able to do this? Get *really* specific! Answer the big "why" it means so much to you.
- You are planning an evening of wonder and awe for somebody special. Who is the evening for? What will be the mode of transportation? What type of attire will you wear? What are your dining plans? Where will you both be going? Why do you want to do this for them?

- Looking back, you realize when you cut one major thing out of your life, you started to see huge benefits. What did you cut out? Why did you decide to remove it from your life? What were the short-term benefits? What were the long-term benefits? What is one piece of advice you'd give somebody who is cutting this from their life now, as a beginner?
- Now that you are entirely healthy, wealthy, and happy, what is one weird thing you do? It could be an elaborate snack, how you dress, a place you go, or anything else!
- Your tax advisor calls and tells you that you must spend $150,000 quickly on business expenses to save money on your taxes. What do you purchase?
- Now that you're happy to your core, what do you find yourself doing more of, simply to enjoy it?
- If you had it to do all over again, what would you do differently because you knew it would help you get back to success the quickest way possible?
- You're sitting on a beautiful overlook, grateful for all you have, all you are, and all you've done. Then, you decide to dare yourself to do something crazy, and it has to be done in 12 hours or less. What do you dare yourself to do and why?
- Since you are uber healthy now, what do you do that you wouldn't have dreamed of doing before becoming healthy?
- You wake up in the middle of the night and head to the kitchen to get some water. You see your loved one sitting at the table - the person you lost a while back and miss terribly. What do they say to you to convey how proud they are of you?
- It's the holiday season! You want to buy gifts for kids who otherwise wouldn't get anything. What age range do you buy for, and what do you get them? Do you have

a special way you give them their presents, or do you donate them anonymously?

· You've got all the time in the world now! So make a plan, for the next 14 days, about something new you're going to try or learn about each day.

· You are planning a vacation that will knock off your socks! Where are you going, how long will you be vacationing, who is going with you, and what will you do once you get there?

· You've learned so much along your journey to becoming all you've ever wanted to be. So what are the top 3 things you can teach others, and why?

· You have absolutely everything you could ever need or want. Make a list of things people can give you for your birthday that you would be overjoyed to receive!

· With all of the personal growth you've accomplished, what are the most significant leaps you've made to become the person you are now, and how did you accomplish those leaps?

· New Year's Day is approaching! Now that you are who you are, living the life you used to dream about, what are your new year's resolutions and why?

· Johnny Appleseed is known for planting apple seeds. Paul Bunyan is known for his strength, speed, and skill. Along those same lines, what are *you* known for and why?

· What small, extravagant thing do you now regularly buy that you would never have imagined buying before you became so wealthy? Why is it so nice to have?

· You decide it's time to give money to family and friends! Who do you give money to, and how much do you give them?

· You've bought everything you've ever wanted, given money to people you have wanted to help, and traveled to the world's far corners. So what do you do with yourself all day?

- You are somewhat an enigma to the people around you who don't quite know you. What makes you so puzzling to them?
- You have *one* message you want to share with the world to help them have the life you now have! What is that message, and how do you deliver it to the masses?
- Write a letter from your future self to your current self, explaining three things you can do right *now* to put you on the path of your dreams.

NOTES, THOUGHTS & IDEAS

_____
_____
_____
_____
_____
_____
_____
_____
_____
_____
_____
_____
_____
_____
_____
_____
_____
_____
_____
_____

Visualization

Visualization is such a valuable tool in becoming all that you could ever dream of becoming! Much like Future Journaling, you visualize yourself as already having achieved what you want in your life.

The benefits of visualizing are only limited to how big your dreams and goals are.

When you visualize, you let your subconscious mind, the Universe, God, your higher self (however you want to look at it) know what you want to happen, and your desire will come into your reality. Quite magical, really.

Tips for visualizing:

- Put as much emotion into your visualization as possible! Imagine and feel happiness, love, joy, and excitement as much as possible!
- Use all of your senses. See yourself jumping with joy, having happy tears, and smiling from ear to ear. Seeing those things will surely allow you to feel the emotions they elicit. Smell the aroma of the falling rain, the bread baking in the oven, or the waft of flowers. Touch your loved ones around you, the medal around your neck, your million dollars, or the infinite amount of different things you could touch. Hear words of gratitude, laughter, music, or crickets in the nighttime. Taste the salty

sea air, the delicious spaghetti, the crisp water, or the flavor of your lip balm. Enliven your visualization with your senses.

· Set a timer. Around 5 minutes of visualization is all you need! Of course, you can go longer if you'd like, but only if you can stay focused on your visualization without your mind wandering.

· Know that you are creating your future when you visualize! Expect what you visualize to come true in your life. This is a simple mindset shift. Allow yourself to believe it, and you will be amazed at your results.

· Know what you're going to visualize before you set your timer. Doing so prevents your mind from wandering and keeps you focused on what you want. You'll see a simple activity on the following pages that will ensure you always know precisely what you will visualize.

NOTES, THOUGHTS & IDEAS

_____
_____
_____
_____
_____
_____
_____
_____
_____
_____
_____
_____
_____
_____
_____
_____
_____
_____
_____
_____
_____
_____
_____
_____

HAPPINESS FACT
Telling somebody you're _unhappy_ can
ease the burden and make you feel happier!

"Live with intention. Walk to the edge. Listen hard.
Practice wellness. Play with abandon. Laugh.
Choose with no regret. Do what you love.
Live as if this is all there is."
~Mary Anne Radmacher-Hershey

NOTES, THOUGHTS & IDEAS

_____
_____
_____
_____
_____
_____
_____
_____
_____
_____
_____
_____
_____
_____
_____
_____
_____
_____
_____
_____
_____

HAPPINESS FACT
Plants and flowers increase your happiness!

Visualization Menu

A Visualization Menu is a piece of paper with different ideas to pick and choose from to visualize. Like at a restaurant, you can see what you like on the menu and pick what sounds good!

To make your menu, you can get as fancy or as practical as you'd like. For example, you can make it look like an actual menu with different headings like health, wealth, utter happiness, family, friends, vacations, where I live, etc.; or you can simply list ideas that you want to visualize.

Below are some questions to get you thinking about what you want on your visualization menu. As you answer them, come up with specific scenarios that excite you! The scenarios don't need to be detailed. You can allow the details to develop as you visualize. You are just looking to set up general situations where you can let your imagination take over during your visualization.

Remember to never insist on these details coming to pass! In allowing something better than your visualizations to happen in your life, you are setting yourself up for incredible surprises. Simply use your visualizations as a time to get excited about your amazing life.

The ideas included below are merely a starting point to get your mind thinking about what would be fantastic for you. Have fun with this because your visualizations are meant to be a great time!

Questions to get you started on your visualization menu:

- You're so healthy! Do you run a 10K, go water skiing, or play with your kids? Perhaps you go to the doctor, and the doctor is amazed that you are healthier than you were last time, or they might even ask what you do to be so healthy that they sit and take notes!
- You're so wealthy! What do you *do* with all of your money? Do you move? Take vacations? Donate to non-profits? What family members and friends do you give money to? What do your financial advisors say to you? What kind of fun do you have with your money?
- Oh, the success! What has made you such a success?! Do you have a business, or do you freelance? Have you written a book, or did you do something to land you in the record books? How do you share your wisdom? What does success mean to you?
- Happiness abounds! What are you doing to feel such happiness?! Do you have large family meals? Paraglide? Scuba Dive? Are you laughing at all of the hilarious movies and plays you can see? Maybe your happiness comes from gardening or organizing a community-wide clean-up!
- Oh, la, la, love! The love you feel is absolutely amazing! Is it with a lifelong partner? Maybe you derive love from the animal shelter or by helping others. What creates love for you? How do you like to express your love? How do you like others to show their love for you?
- Vacations galore! Where do you want to go on vacation? How will you get there, and what will you do once you arrive? Who do you go with?
- Home sweet home! Exactly what do you want your home to be? A single-story, two-story or more? Do you want to be in the country or maybe a condo above some shops in

a small town? Is your home warm and inviting or modern and sleek? Do you have a lot of windows? Do you have a great view? What are your wonderful neighbors like, and how close are they? Is your community connected, or do you all keep your distance?

Those are the main categories that most people visualize, but your imagination is the limit (which means there *is no limit*) to what you can visualize and have in your life. So go crazy and list all the goodies you think you could possibly want. There are no wrong answers here - you can visualize anything you want!

If you go to ErinChavez.com/FGTHBonus, you'll find a sample visualization menu available as a free download!

NOTES, THOUGHTS & IDEAS

_____

_____

_____

_____

_____

_____

_____

_____

_____

_____

_____

_____

_____

_____

_____

_____

_____

_____

_____

_____

_____

Planning

Planning is an old-school tool, but it can help you get your footing and take off running! We all know the chances of us snapping our fingers and achieving our goals are unlikely. Not because it isn't possible (*anything* is possible), but because we don't *believe* it's possible. What we *do* believe is possible is working in a direction toward what we want to get what we want. That's where planning comes into play.

Planning can be a straightforward process, and it is literally as fun as you make it out to be.

Steps to planning:

- Pick your ultimate goal.
- Come up with 3-5 mini-goals to get you to your ultimate goal.
- For each of the 3-5 mini-goals, come up with 3-5 micro-goals or to-do's that will help you achieve the mini-goals.
- From the goals you create, do *something* toward those goals every day.
- Have fun working on those goals, knowing your ultimate goal is on the other side.
- Do a short, daily visualization of you living your life *after* accomplishing your goal.

Planning Example

Here's an example of planning your goal:

Ultimate Goal: Vacation in Paris!

Mini-Goals

- Make travel accommodations and know where I want to go and what I want to see.
- Save $10,000 for a spectacular trip (including things to take with me)!
- Prepare for the trip and the care of my pets & home for my time away.

Mini-Goal: Make travel accommodations and know where I want to go and what I want to see.

- Research the area, tour the area on google maps and look up reviews of the possibilities.
- See if there is a group tour I might be interested in (that provides discounts!)
- Prepare for the trip (find passport!) and find someone to take care of my pets while I'm vacationing.

Mini-Goal: Save $10k for a spectacular trip (including things to take with me)!

- Budget my current money and save as much as possible.
- Look for and do side gigs, and all of that income goes toward my trip.
- Look for travel discounts so my money will go further.

Mini-Goal: Prepare for the trip and the care of my pets & home while I'm vacationing.

- Look for a reliable pet sitter that will also water my plants and bring in my mail.
- Go shopping for my trip! (Remember good walking shoes!)
- Make sure all my bills will be paid while I'm in Paris.

Make weekly to-do lists based on your mini-goals, cross something off every day, and visualize daily!

NOTES, THOUGHTS & IDEAS

_____
_____
_____
_____
_____
_____
_____
_____
_____
_____
_____
_____
_____
_____
_____
_____
_____
_____
_____
_____

QUOTE

"Your outside world is a reflection of your inside world.
What goes on on the inside shows on the outside."
~ Bob Proctor

NOTES, THOUGHTS & IDEAS

_____

_____

_____

_____

_____

_____

_____

_____

_____

_____

_____

_____

_____

_____

_____

_____

_____

_____

_____

_____

REMEMBER

On social media, tag pictures of you
being happy with #fgthbook.
We will build our Happiness Family!

Feel Your Way

While this is a very simple practice, it will undoubtedly change your life for the better! It's all about feeling your way to the happy life you desire.

Let's say you want to be a famous illustrator. Spend your day as a famous illustrator!

In your mind, what does a famous illustrator do on a day-to-day basis? Chances are, they do a lot of the same things you are currently doing. They wake up, shower, have some coffee, eat, go grocery shopping, and illustrate something in their studio.

The key to feeling your way is much like when a child plays make-believe. Like a child who pretends to be a princess or a cowboy, you pretend to be a famous illustrator! Your words, thoughts, the way you carry yourself, what you research during the day, how you spend your free time... all of it is as if you are a famous illustrator!

Honestly, one of the best things about doing this is when you're at the store. You walk around thinking, "Do these people know who I am?!" It's like you have a little secret because you are (your name), THE famous illustrator! (Let it be known that this should be done humbly and not with a pompous nature.)

Once you do this one time, you will probably get hooked pretty quickly. Then, you can start looking for little things you can buy to help you play out this role more and more. For example, just like a child playing a cowboy would thoroughly enjoy having a cowboy hat, a famous illustrator might enjoy having a smock. Or perhaps you envision a famous illustrator wearing ripped jeans and an old t-shirt. Whatever your character looks like to you, see how you can spruce it up with props.

When you feel your way towards the person you want to be, you live out the grandest visualization! You are putting it out there that *you are* who you want to be.

And on a deeper level, you are also convincing yourself. That is one of the most important things you can do.

NOTES, THOUGHTS & IDEAS

_____
_____
_____
_____
_____
_____
_____
_____
_____
_____
_____
_____
_____
_____
_____
_____
_____
_____
_____
_____

NOTES, THOUGHTS & IDEAS

_____
_____
_____
_____
_____
_____
_____
_____
_____
_____
_____
_____
_____
_____
_____
_____
_____
_____
_____
_____
_____
_____

Self Expression

What is life for if you do not express your individuality? We are here to be happy and to soar! Being true to yourself is vital, and when you do this, you will free your spirit in a way that is impossible with any other practice. Essentially, self-expression is the expression of your personality, beliefs, and feelings.

We are so conditioned by society to what we are supposed to do and what we are supposed to look like. It is time to release yourself from those shackles and allow yourself to soar!

Allowing yourself to be you might take some thought on your part. After all, we often bury that side of us so others don't think we are "weird." If you don't know how to express yourself, give yourself a little time to uncover the true you. Once you start, it will happen quickly!

Perhaps you already know who you truly are and how you want to express yourself. That is fantastic! You simply need to give yourself permission to let her out and explore this life the way you are meant to.

So, are you ready to feel fantastic and free?!

Examples of Self Expression:

- Hairstyle and color
- Choice of clothes
- Choice of words
- Artistic expression

- Musical expression
- How you walk
- How you talk
- How you dance
- What you write
- What you share
- The stories you tell yourself
- The stories you tell others
- Who you support
- What you *want* from life
- What you choose to believe
- What you choose to talk about

For the sake of humanity, please embrace yourself and express yourself in ways that feel awesome to you for the sake of your well-being!

And just like your mama told ya — if people don't like the real you, they aren't your kind of people.

NOTES, THOUGHTS & IDEAS

_____

_____
_____
_____
_____
_____
_____
_____
_____
_____
_____
_____
_____
_____
_____
_____
_____
_____
_____
_____
_____
_____
_____
_____

NOTES, THOUGHTS & IDEAS

_____
_____
_____
_____
_____
_____
_____
_____
_____
_____
_____
_____
_____
_____
_____
_____
_____
_____

Gratitude

If you've never kept a gratitude list or journal, it most often starts with the obvious things in life. We're grateful for the ones we love, our homes, the incredible meal we had the night prior, and other basic, ordinary things in our lives. Not that there's anything wrong with those things! They are all excellent and are perfect reasons to feel gratitude!

However, the more you list what you are grateful for, you will begin to open your eyes to the magic of life. You'll realize just how grateful you are for the way that leaf spun in the wind and made you smile, or how you're grateful that you were able to sit and simply be, enjoying the breeze on your face for a few minutes that day. The little things in life will become the big things, and you will wonder how you ever lived without noticing them before.

Don't think you can only be grateful for things in the past or present. You can even be grateful for the things you want in your future. Every single thing in this world began with a thought. Think about what you want in your future, and it is already created. Be thankful for that thing, be grateful that it has been created and is coming to you.

There are many benefits to including gratitude in your daily life:

- Decreases stress.
- Helps with depression and anxiety.
- Opens our eyes to more and more things to enjoy and be grateful for.
- Allows us to be more positive in general.
- Helps to improve health.
- Improves the quality of our lives overall.
- Sleep better.
- Have more energy.
- Feel better about ourselves.
- Find happiness *within* ourselves rather than outside of ourselves.

To incorporate gratitude, simply write down (or think of) 3-5 reasons you have to be grateful each day. The longer you practice gratitude, the easier it will become, and the more your life will change for the better.

The bottom line is that we are here to experience life! Therefore, everything we experience is something to be grateful for because it is something we can enjoy or learn and grow from.

QUOTE

"Gratitude is the single most important ingredient
to living a successful and fulfilled life."
~ Jack Canfield

NOTES, THOUGHTS & IDEAS

_____
_____
_____
_____
_____
_____
_____
_____
_____
_____
_____
_____
_____
_____
_____
_____
_____
_____
_____
_____
_____

REMEMBER

On social media, tag pictures of you
being happy with **#fgthbook**.
We will build our Happiness Family!

NOTES, THOUGHTS & IDEAS

_____

_____

_____

_____

_____

_____

_____

_____

_____

_____

_____

_____

_____

_____

_____

_____

_____

_____

_____

Section 4 - Reference

Sometimes to feel happy, we just need to be reminded of some fantastic resources we have on this earth. That's what this section is all about. You probably know most of what is listed here, but to have it in one spot will make it easy to refer to, so you can remind yourself of the power available to you, and so you can create your own activities that will create happiness in your life!

Emotions Chart

When you know where you are, you know where to go; and that's exactly what this chart is designed to help you with! If you're feeling depressed, you can't expect yourself to jump to feeling happy automatically. There are steps in between, and each step feels a little better and a little better. This chart will show you the way.

Energy & Vibration

Everything in our world vibrates, even if it appears to be solid or if it is simply the air around you. I'm sure you've walked into someplace and noticed it had "bad vibes" or "good vibes." There are ways you can manipulate your energy and the energy around you, so you can create good vibes whenever you'd like.

Universal Laws

Universal Laws have been proven by science to be true in the past, the present, and the future. They simply are truths of the Universe. Therefore, when we study, understand, and implement these laws, we can work with them, making our lives easier.

Chakras

Chakras are rotating energy centers located in the body. You have as many as 114 chakras, but they all belong to 7 main chakras. You will be able to refer to this section to learn about your seven main chakras, what they mean, and how to make them spin optimally. Your life will be balanced when your chakras are lined up and spinning well.

Divination

Are you ready to learn about some of the easiest divination tools?! Oracle cards, automatic writing, pendulums, and stichomancy will be covered. If you find one that speaks to you and you have a natural inclination for it, nurture it and grow with its use! Divination is fun and can give you answers that you didn't know you had.

Recommended Reading

While many books can help you along your happiness path, the books listed in this section have significantly impacted me. They will educate and motivate you to be happy and know your innate power. When we realize the power we each hold, life becomes the game it is meant to be!

NOTES, THOUGHTS & IDEAS

_____
_____
_____
_____
_____
_____
_____
_____
_____
_____
_____
_____
_____
_____
_____
_____
_____
_____
_____
_____

NOTES, THOUGHTS & IDEAS

_____

_____

_____

_____

_____

_____

_____

_____

_____

_____

_____

_____

_____

_____

_____

_____

_____

_____

_____

_____

Emotions Chart

When you see where you are and what you're feeling, you will know your next step to feeling better. That's exactly what this chart is designed to help you with. If you're feeling depressed, you can't expect yourself to jump to feeling happy automatically. There are steps in between, and each step feels a little better and a little better.

Sometimes the amount of time it takes to get from one emotion to another is relatively quick — it might take minutes for you. Other times, it can be a lengthy process. If that happens, don't beat yourself up. Instead, give yourself the love you deserve for caring enough about yourself to put in the effort to work your way up the emotions chart. Also, it's possible to feel happy in most areas of your life, except for one thing that always makes you feel not happy. It is perfectly normal to feel happy while working on something that doesn't feel great. In fact, so many areas of your life will improve simply because you worked through the emotions of something that wasn't sitting right with you.

How do you work your way up the emotions chart? It is totally up to you, and there are no wrong answers. We'll go over some ways that might feel good to you with that in mind.

Sit and think. With your chart in front of you, think about if you can move up the emotions simply by thinking them through. Sometimes it just takes some rational thinking without the emotions behind it.

Journaling helps you work through your emotions so well. For example, if you feel disappointed by something, write about why you are disappointed. Then assess and see if overwhelm or frustration is what you're feeling after writing. If it is, write about why you feel that way next.

Get out and do something. Some of us dwell upon our negative situations. If that is the case with you, get out of your head for a while and do something different. This works best if you do something you have to focus on, so your thoughts can't be on your negative situation.

Do something for somebody else. Helping others, or doing something nice for them, can put things in perspective for you and help make you feel better.

The old standbys. Turning to things like gratitude, prayer, meditation, ho'oponopono, exercise, cleaning, decluttering, and other similar activities can help you work through what you're going through simply by improving your mood overall. When we're feeling bad and flood ourselves with goodness, it does so much good.

You are so worthy of feeling happy! Take the time to give yourself that gift.

You can download a free, full-color Emotions chart at Erin-Chavez.com/FGTHBonus.

JOY/APPRECIIATION/EMPOWERMENT/FREEDOM/LOVE

PASSION

ENTHUSIASM/EXCITEMENT/HAPPINESS

POSITIVE EXPECTATION/UNFAILING BELIEF

OPTIMISM/HOPEFULNESS

CONTENTMENT

BOREDOM

PESSIMISM

FRUSTRATION/IRRITATION/IMPATIENCE

OVERWHELMENT

DISAPPOINTMENT

DOUBT

WORRY

BLAME

DISCOURAGEMENT

ANGER/REVENGE

HATRED/RAGE

JEALOUSY

INSECURITY/GUILT/UNWORTHINESS

FEAR/GRIEF/DESPAIR/POWERLESSNESS/VICTIM

EMOTIONS CHART

NOTES, THOUGHTS & IDEAS

_____
_____
_____
_____
_____
_____
_____
_____
_____
_____
_____
_____
_____
_____
_____
_____
_____
_____
_____
_____
_____

Energy and
Vibration

Everything in our world vibrates, even if it appears to be solid or if it is simply the air around you. You've surely walked into a place or met somebody and noticed either *bad vibes* or *good vibes*.

Sometimes the energy of another person or place can be enough to lower *your* vibration, so if you feel somebody or someplace is getting you down, get away from them or leave the area! Then, immediately do something that will make you feel better after you're gone.

It's all about manipulating *your* energy and the energy around you.

First and foremost, the entirety of this book is designed to raise your vibration. When you're happy, your vibration is high. So flip through this guide, find something that feels good to you, and do it.

Here are some other ideas to feel better after encountering negative energy/vibes or to protect your own:

1. Physically shake your arms and legs to get the negative energy off your body.
2. Wear a special necklace (like amethyst and clear quartz) to keep negative energy at bay and protect your energy.

3. Try tapping, also known as The Emotional Freedom Technique. (Pioneered by Gary Craig.)
4. Learn about feng shui and implement its practices in your home, car, and office.
5. Have plants that raise vibration like basil, bamboo, succulents, jade, and roses.

Your thoughts also have their own vibes, and they might be the most important vibes to pay attention to.

Constantly being aware of your thoughts is almost impossible, but if you have a reminder set to check in on your thoughts regularly, you will learn the trend of your thoughts. Are they more positive or more negative? As humans, we are wired to have more negative thoughts. It goes back to early human days when fight or flight was crucial to our survival. Things have evolved, though, so we also need to evolve our natural thought processes. We do this by choosing happiness in our lives and creating circumstances where happiness is the natural by-product.

It is essential to know that we invite negativity into our lives when our thoughts are negative. Luckily, the opposite is also true. Positive thoughts will attract positivity into our lives. Our dreams, goals, and happiness depend on our good vibe thoughts.

A great way to know if your thoughts are trending positive or negative is to look at different areas of your life, like your health, finances, relationships, etc. Take note of how those are going for you. If you don't like where they are, you have negative thoughts surrounding them. If you like how they are going, you have positive thoughts about them.

Remember that your thoughts carry vibrations and like attracts like. Therefore, you want to strive for good thoughts, so your life will go the way you want. This is precisely why happiness is the language of life.

Music and Energy

Another way to influence your vibration is a particular type of music based on the **Ancient Solfeggio Scale**.

You can find free downloads of the Ancient Solfeggio Scale at ErinChavez.com/FGTHBonus.

This scale was discovered by a Benedictine monk known as Guido D'Arezzo. He said that each scale is mathematically in tune with the universe and has different energetic properties.

396 HZ

Turn grief into joy and unblock subconscious blocks that have led to current negative situations.

417 HZ

Produces energy that will encourage change in your life with help from an ever-flowing source of energy (God, the Universe, etc.) It will also cleanse past trauma and encourage your cells to function optimally.

528 HZ

Will return DNA to its perfect state, bring transformation and miracles to you, and increase your energy, peace, intuition, and creativity.

639 HZ

Creates harmonious relationships and enhances tolerance, communication, and love.

741 HZ

Helps to solve any type of problem, gives you the gift of self-expression, and helps you live a simpler and healthier life.

852 HZ

Opens your mind, body, and heart up to communication with your higher self, angels, the Universe, God, and those deceased.

936 HZ

Connects you to your personal source. Awakens intuition, and connection to the spiritual world.

Binaural Beats are yet another type of music used to change your vibration. Binaural beats work by pulsating music that will encourage your brain to sync up to its pulsing sounds so you can achieve a desired result. This music must be listened to via headphones.

(Binaural Beats are not for people with epilepsy because they could cause seizures due to the brain wave change.)
You can find free binaural beat downloads at ErinChavez.com/FGTHBonus.

Delta .5-4HZ

Encourages deep sleep. Your awareness is fully detached. Being in Delta is excellent for healing.

Theta 4 - 7.5HZ

For deep meditation and REM sleep. Great for visualizing. Being in Theta lowers stress and anxiety.

Alpha 7.5 - 14HZ

For relaxation and meditation. Great for learning new information. Being in Alpha allows your mind to work optimally, with focus, without the distraction of overactive thoughts.

Beta 14 - 40HZ

Normal state of mind while awake. Great for being alert. Being in Beta is terrific for focus and critical reasoning.

Gamma 40HZ and above

For intense focus and problem-solving. Great for memorization. Gamma brain waves are present while you are in the zone and fully focused on what you are doing. Creativity and happiness flow freely while in Gamma.

"Tension is who you think you should be;
relaxation is who you are."
~ Chinese Proverb

NOTES, THOUGHTS & IDEAS

_____
_____
_____
_____
_____
_____
_____
_____
_____
_____
_____
_____
_____
_____
_____
_____
_____
_____
_____
_____
_____

HAPPINESS FACT
Spending time alone can make you
more creative *and* happier!

NOTES, THOUGHTS & IDEAS

_____
_____
_____
_____
_____
_____
_____
_____
_____
_____
_____
_____
_____
_____
_____
_____
_____
_____
_____
_____

Universal Laws

Universal Laws are facts of life that quantum physics has proved. They are true if you believe in them or not, just like gravity -they simply are how things work. When we study, understand, and implement these laws, we can work with them, and our lives will be so much easier.

Law of Vibration

Each and every thing has a vibration, unique to itself. Every material thing vibrates, and every thought, feeling, and desire vibrates. When your thoughts correspond with a matching vibration, it will draw that matched vibration into your life.

Law of Attraction

We attract things, events, and people that come into our lives based on the vibration of our thoughts, feelings, and desires. Positive attracts positive, and negative attracts negative.

Law of Divine Oneness

We are all connected. Everything we think, say, do, and believe affects not only our own energy but the people/situations around us and the world as well.

Law of Compensation
This law shows that we are rewarded with gifts, money, friendships, and blessings based on our contributions to others.

Law of Polarity
Everything has an opposite. If we have unwanted thoughts or circumstances, we can focus on the opposite to improve our situation. This is the law of mental vibrations.

Law of Correspondence
Whatever laws of physics we have on earth, there are corresponding laws of the universe. So you can look to our physical world for answers about how the Universe works.

Law of Inspired Action
We must take action toward what we want. The action can be small or large, but we must take those steps to get what we want and do things that support our desires.

Law of Cause and Effect
This law states that everything that happens in our lives is based on Universal Laws. Therefore, anything we think has an effect.

Law of Relativity
Everything is relative. If we are faced with a situation, there is another better situation and another worse one. This law also says that we must stay connected to our hearts and stay faithful in our thoughts to receive what we want — because we always receive what we think about.

Law of Gender

Everything, including ourselves, has both feminine and masculine properties. Masculine energies are more ego-centered, and feminine energies are more spirit-centered. For true creation, we must incorporate both energies into our lives.

Law of Perpetual Transmutation of Energy

This law proves that you have the power to change your life. We simply need to adhere to these Universal Laws.

Law of Rhythm

Everything on earth has a cycle. The seasons, the tide, the moon phases — they all repeat themselves endlessly. So likewise, things will cycle back to going well again when things are not going as planned. The key is to acknowledge this fact and keep all disappointments and excitement relative to the situation.

NOTES, THOUGHTS & IDEAS

_____

_____

_____

_____

_____

_____

_____

_____

_____

_____

_____

_____

_____

_____

_____

_____

_____

_____

_____

NOTES, THOUGHTS & IDEAS

_____
_____
_____
_____
_____
_____
_____
_____
_____
_____
_____
_____
_____
_____
_____
_____
_____
_____
_____

Chakras

Chakras are rotating energy centers located in the body. You have as many as 114 chakras, but they all belong to 7 main chakras. You will be able to refer to this section to learn about your seven main chakras, what they mean, and how to make them spin optimally. Your life will be balanced when your chakras are lined up and spinning well.

You will find specific information for each chakra:
Color
Location
Food
Stones
Essential Oils
Frequency (See *Energy & Vibration* for more info.)
Main Focus of Chakra
Positive Aspects
Malfunctioning Chakra
Affirmations

With this knowledge, you will know if your chakra is spinning correctly or if there is work to be done on the chakra. You can make this work as complicated or as simple as you desire. It all has to do with the intent you give.

For example, if you tell yourself that eating a banana each day will balance your 3rd chakra, it will. Or, if you'd like to get more into it, you could take a bath with basil oil sprinkled in, a tiger's eye stone to meditate with and a ginger candle burning beside your bath. Either way is right, and either way is okay and appropriate. It all depends on what you want to do.

You can find Magic Recipes for your chakras in Section One.

Chakra Check-In

Below is a quick and general check-in to see if you have a chakra in immediate need of care.

Are you feeling anxious, non-connected, unable to trust, or insecure? *Go to the root chakra.*

Are you feeling standoffish, fearful, depressed, uninspired, or unstable? *Go to the sacral chakra.*

Are you feeling irresponsible, have low self-esteem, or are unable to make decisions or reach goals? *Go to the solar plexus chakra.*

Are you feeling shy, lonely, unable to love, forgive, or show compassion? *Go to the heart chakra.*

Are you feeling it difficult to speak your truth, have conversations, or express yourself? *Go to the throat chakra.*

Are you feeling little imagination, not clear on your thoughts or what you want to do with your life, or unable to focus? *Go to the third eye chakra.*

Are you feeling self-destructive, overwhelmed, confused, isolated, or have issues with trust? *Go to the crown chakra.*

Root Chakra

Color
Red

Location
Base of spine

Food
Red apples, tomatoes, strawberries, beets - red foods.
Sweet potatoes, potatoes, onions, ginger, garlic - root vegetables.

Stones
Garnet, Hematite, Tourmaline, Bloodstone, Ruby

Essential Oils
Patchouli, Sandalwood

Frequency
396 HZ

Main Focus
Basic Trust/Physical Existence

Functioning Chakra

Feeling supported, connected, grounded, and safe in your physical world. Stability, vitality, patience, and tenacity are strong in a well-balanced root chakra.

Malfunctioning Chakra

Feelings of fear around money, shelter, food, and providing for life's basic necessities. Poor boundaries, trouble letting go, fear, and anxiety. Also, problems with the lower part of your body, including the: legs, feet, rectum, tailbone, and lower back, point to a malfunctioning root chakra. General sluggishness.

How to Balance

Take care of your physical life and focus on being human. Walk barefoot, dance, visualize red at the base of your spine, and incorporate the foods, stones, essential oils, and frequency listed above.

Affirmations

I am stable, safe, and strong.
I am secure and grounded in my life.
I am good at living my life.

Sacral Chakra

Color
Orange

Location
Two inches below the belly button

Food
Oranges, sweet potatoes, mangos, carrots, peaches - orange foods.

Stones
Moonstone, Citrine, Gold, Peach Aventurine

Essential Oils
Jasmine, Geranium, Orange

Frequency
417 HZ

Main Focus
Sexuality/Creativity/Feeling good in your own skin

Functioning Chakra
Taking positive risks, being creative, being committed. Feeling playful, sexual, outgoing, abundant, free with emotions.

Malfunctioning Chakra

Issues with commitment, inability to play and have fun, issues with sex, impotence, and addiction. There are also issues with the reproductive system, menstrual, urinary, and kidney dysfunctions.

How to Balance

Stretch your hips, journal about your feelings (especially feelings about your sexuality and creativity), visualize orange 2" below the belly button, and incorporate the foods, stones, essential oils, and frequency listed above.

Affirmations

I am a creative being, and it flows out of me.
I am a sexual being, and it feels natural.
I enjoy the pleasures that life has to offer.

Solar Plexus Chakra

Color
Yellow

Location
Stomach area

Food
Lemons, bananas, pineapple, corn, whole grains - yellow foods.

Stones
Topaz, Citrine, Tiger's Eye

Essential Oils
Lemon, Basil, Ginger

Frequency
528 HZ

Main Focus
Self Acceptance/Wisdom/Power/Confidence

Functioning Chakra
Feeling powerful, confident, humorous, in control, optimistic, calm, and mental clarity. Acceptance of others and self.

Malfunctioning Chakra

Digestive issues, high blood pressure, diabetes, stomach issues, nervousness, and low energy. Negative self-talk, low self-esteem, and need to purchase material items.

How to Balance

Spend time in the sun, spend time with people who adore you, notice when you talk poorly of yourself, visualize yellow around your stomach area, and incorporate the foods, stones, essential oils, and frequency listed above.

Affirmations

I am confident and powerful!
I laugh often.
I am sure of myself.

Heart Chakra

Color
Green

Location
Heart area

Food
Cucumbers, leafy greens, avocados, broccoli, kiwi - green foods.

Stones
Rose Quartz, Jade, Emerald, Green Aventurine, Malachite

Essential Oils
Sandalwood, Rose, Ylang Ylang, Frankincense

Frequency
639 HZ

Main Focus
Love/Healing/Compassion

Functioning Chakra
Feelings of love, joy, peace, gratitude, wholeness, compassion, and balance. Forgiveness & trust are easy.

Malfunctioning Chakra

Issues with the heart and lungs. Jealousy, bitterness, lonesomeness. Unable to accept or give love freely, be generous, or follow your passions.

How to Balance

Correct your posture, write yourself love letters, follow your dreams, volunteer, visualize green in your heart area, and incorporate the foods, stones, essential oils, and frequency listed above.

Affirmations

I am pure love.

I am so grateful that _____.

I spread love around the world.

Throat Chakra

Color
Blue

Location
Throat area

Food
Blueberries, blue raspberries - blue foods.
Honey, hot teas - things that soothe your throat.

Stones
Amazonite, Turquoise, Aquamarine, Blue Lace Agate

Essential Oils
Peppermint, Basil, Eucalyptus, Lavender

Frequency
741 HZ

Main Focus
Verbal Communication/Self-Expression

Functioning Chakra
Easily able to express desires, thoughts, and inner voice.
Honesty, feeling heard, and good listening skills.

Malfunctioning Chakra

Fearful of no power or choice. Unable to speak up on important matters, express concerns, or believe in your creativity. Fearful of being judged and challenging to be in silence. Also, issues with sore throats, ear infections, and pain in the neck/shoulders.

How to Balance

Sing loud and proud! Be open and honest with yourself and others. If you have trouble speaking to somebody, shower them in love (in your imagination), visualize blue in your throat, and incorporate the foods, stones, essential oils, and frequency listed above.

Affirmations

I know my truth, and I share it freely.
I say what I feel.
I am allowed my own opinion.

Third Eye Chakra

Color
Purple

Location
Between Eyebrows

Food
Blackberries, purple grapes, plums, eggplant, purple potatoes - purple foods.

Stones
Amethyst, Sodalite, Obsidian, Labradorite

Essential Oils
Clary Sage, Rosemary, Ylang Ylang, Lavender

Frequency
852 HZ

Main Focus
See the Big Picture/Awareness

Functioning Chakra

Feelings of clarity, focus, insight, imagination, and con-nectedness. A power to perceive the world as it truly is (pure love) and to heal and love freely.

Malfunctioning Chakra

Headaches, moodiness, sinus issues, eye, and ear problems. Also afraid to look at our problems or to face our fears. Worry, anxiety and confusion.

How to Balance

Look for deeper meanings in what you hear and see. Sense the vibrations around you and decide if they are good or bad. Celebrate when your intuition is correct, visualize purple in between your eyebrows and incorporate the foods, stones, essential oils, and frequency listed above.

Affirmations

I am calm and peaceful.
I intuitively know the correct answer.
I follow my inner guidance.

Crown Chakra

Color
Indigo

Location
Top of Head

Food
Water

Stones
Clear Quartz, Selenite, White Agate, Diamond

Essential Oils
Myrrh, Violet, Frankincense, Rose, Sandalwood

Frequency
963HZ

Main Focus
Connection to Spirit/Universe/God

Functioning Chakra
Feelings of complete connectedness, oneness with All, bliss, knowing. Complete trust in our true selves and inner guidance.

Malfunctioning Chakra

Rigid thoughts, inability to get out of your head, prejudices, analysis paralysis, confusion. Depression, migraines, skin disorders, dizziness, learning disabilities.

How to Balance

Get fresh air and sunlight. Meditate, be inspired in a way that feels good to you, visualize indigo at the crown of your head, and incorporate water and the stones, essential oils, and frequency listed above.

Affirmations

I am connected. I am one with everything.
I have endless ideas that serve me and humanity.
I am...

NOTES, THOUGHTS & IDEAS

_____
_____
_____
_____
_____
_____
_____
_____
_____
_____
_____
_____
_____
_____
_____
_____
_____
_____
_____
_____
_____
_____
_____

"Always remember the answers come not from the rock,
the teacup, the shell, or the cards.
The answers come from you."
~ Gwendolyn Womack

NOTES, THOUGHTS & IDEAS

_____
_____
_____
_____
_____
_____
_____
_____
_____
_____
_____
_____
_____
_____
_____
_____
_____
_____
_____
_____
_____

HAPPINESS FACT
Carpe Diem! Live for the day,
and you will be happier for doing so!

Divination

Divination is using various methods to discover hidden knowledge by using intuitive perception. While some people see this as a psychic with scarves, incense, and a dimly lit room, there are much easier ways to use divination, and no crystal balls are required.

Are you ready to learn about some of the easiest divination tools?! Oracle cards, automatic writing, pendulums, and stichomancy will be covered. If you find one that speaks to you and you have a natural inclination for it, nurture it and grow with its use! Divination is fun and can give you answers that you didn't know you had.

A note about tarot cards: Tarot cards are different from oracle cards and are also an excellent tool for divination. Tarot cards have precise meanings for each card, so the reader's intuition isn't utilized *as much* as in the other methods listed below. However, they can be a reliable form of divination if you are drawn to tarot. The other methods that will be covered are based solely on intuition, with no predisposed meanings.

Oracle Cards

Oracle cards are a deck of cards with different images on them. As you may have seen above, regarding the tarot cards, different layouts can get different answers. For example, perhaps you will have three piles. One is for the past, present, and future, or the three piles could mean three months from now, six months from now, and one year from now. The options are endless.

A one-card draw is also a popular way to use oracle cards. The deck is shuffled, a card is picked (or falls out), and you can use that card as a journaling prompt, an intention for the day, or a quick answer to a question.

A lot of oracle decks have a word or phrase on the card. You can use that word or phrase to kickstart your intuition, or you can simply look at the images on the cards and use your intuition for the meaning behind the card.

Always go with your first instinct when reading oracle cards.

Automatic Writing

Automatic writing is when you put your pen on paper and wait for it to start moving, writing out messages from the spirit realm. This can be a slow start for some people, but the more you attempt automatic writing, the quicker it will become. You can start by writing a question and then waiting for an answer to be written, or simply put your pen down and wait.

You can ask to talk to a loved one or a famous person who has passed away, your guardian angel, your higher self, your future self, and really anybody you'd like to hear from.

Automatic writing is an enjoyable and safe method of divination, but it is best practice to surround yourself with white light before starting automatic writing. You are, after all, opening yourself to the spirit side of life.

You will know you are communicating with desirable spirits when your messages are filled with love because pure love is what they are.

Pendulums

It is up to debate if pendulums move based on our subconscious knowledge, inducing microscopic muscle movement in our fingers, or if the pendulum moves due to a more spiritual nature. Whichever it is, it doesn't matter because you will get accurate results when you use a pendulum.

A beautiful pendulum is very lovely to use, but you could simply use a necklace with a somewhat weighted charm or stone on it as well. You can even get a string and tie something heavier at the bottom and use that for a pendulum.

Hold the top of the chain or string between your thumb and finger and rest your hand at your third eye (between your eyebrows). Ask for the pendulum to show you "yes." It will move in a specific direction. Ask for it to show you a "no." It will move in a different direction. After determining your yes and no directions, you can start asking questions.

Generally, people have quicker success with pendulums than with automatic writing; but the more you practice using a pendulum, the quicker it will become. (With more prominent movements too!)

Stichomancy

Stichomancy might be one of the oldest divination practices, dating back at least 3000 years. It is simply having a question, picking a random book, opening to a random page, and pointing to a place on the page. Then, you read that part of the page and interpret the answer according to your question.

Sometimes the paragraph you point to may seem not to apply at all! That's okay. Allow your answer to form in your mind. Intuition plays a massive role in stichomancy, so building your intuition by practicing this method daily is recommended. Plus, it's a lot of fun!

QUOTE

"There is something really amazing about you. Your unique ideas and thoughts that you bring to this world. Your smile, your laugh... It's you, and you are valuable, worthy, and cherished."
~ Rachel Hamilton

NOTES, THOUGHTS & IDEAS

_____
_____
_____
_____
_____
_____
_____
_____
_____
_____
_____
_____
_____
_____
_____
_____
_____
_____
_____
_____

HAPPINESS FACT

Having sex once a week will lead to optimal happiness!

NOTES, THOUGHTS & IDEAS

In Conclusion

Do you know what a magnificent person you are? Do you know what power you hold? I sure hope you do because you will live a life beyond your wildest dreams when you embrace this magical part of you.

Giving yourself to this magical side of life all begins with your happiness. When you are *happy*, all the other parts of life seem to fall into place. Your thoughts, your actions, your beliefs... When you're happy, they are all good. When your thoughts, actions, and beliefs are good, the world opens up and becomes your playground.

I will do whatever I can to help you on your happiness journey. Please contact me and let me know how to be of service to you. ErinChavez.com/Contact

Also, you would help a *lot* if you'd leave a review where you purchased this book. The more reviews this book receives, the more people it can help, and the more people this book helps, more and more happiness will circulate through this world. (If you forget where you purchased, you can send a review to ErinChavez.com/Contact.)

To your growing happiness,
Erin
Happiness is the Language of Life

You can find social media links, other products, upcoming books, and more at ErinChavez.com.

You might also enjoy the companion book:
Field Guide to Happiness Journal: A Journal to Record What Makes You Happy.

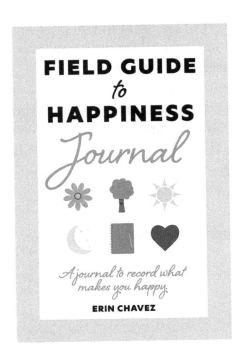

Recommended Reading

While many books can help you along your happiness path, the books listed in this section have significantly impacted me personally. They will educate and motivate you to be happy and know your innate power. When we realize the power we each hold, life becomes the game it is meant to be!

Leveraging the Universe by Mike Dooley

The Power of Your Subconscious Mind by Dr. Joseph Murphy

Ask and It is Given by Esther and Jerry Hicks

The Course in Miracles Experiment by Pam Grout

The Four Agreements by don Miguel Ruiz

Love Money Money Loves You by Sarah McCrum

The Tapping Solution for Manifesting Your Greatest Self by Nick Ortner

Your Invisible Power by Genevieve Behrend

E-Squared by Pam Grout

Write it Down, Make it Happen by Henriette Anne Klauser

Playing the Matrix by Mike Dooley

The Magic Mala by Bob Olson

The Strangest Secret by Earl Nightingale

Acres of Diamonds by Russell H. Conwell

The Alchemist by Paulo Coelho

It Works by RHJ

NOTES, THOUGHTS & IDEAS

_____
_____
_____
_____
_____
_____
_____
_____
_____
_____
_____
_____
_____
_____
_____
_____
_____
_____
_____